**PRINT CASEBOOKS 10/
THE BEST IN ADVERTISING**

PRINT
CASEBOOKS 10
THE BEST IN
ADVERTISING

Written by
Joyce Rutter Kaye
Published by
RC Publications, Inc., Rockville, MD

Introduction

First published in 1994 in the United States of America by RC Publications, Inc. 3200 Tower Oaks Boulevard Rockville, MD 20852

Manufactured in Singapore

First Printing 1994

PRINT CASEBOOKS 10/THE BEST IN ADVERTISING (1994–95 EDITION)
Library of Congress Catalog Card Number 75-649581
ISBN 0-915734-88-5

PRINT CASEBOOKS 10 (1994–95 EDITION)
Complete 6-Volume Set
ISBN 0-915734-87-7

RC PUBLICATIONS
President and Publisher: Howard Cadel
Vice President and Editor: Martin Fox
Managing Director: Linda Silver
Art Director: Andrew P. Kner
Assistant Art Director:
Michele L. Trombley
Copy Editor: Sue Scarfe
Cover Illustration: Brian Ajhar

What are creative people in the advertising community concerned about today? The answer has little to do with the information superhighway, new media, fragmented audiences, interactive television, CD-ROMs, infomercials, the diminished value of the traditional 30-second network commercial, and the diminished value of the traditional advertising agency.

The 45 creative directors, art directors, and copywriters interviewed for this Casebook were less concerned with shaping a message to fit the confines of a new medium than about finding better ways to connect with consumers using powerful and relevant messages. Sure, this group has been chanting this mantra for years, but the difference is that today there is an almost desperate urgency in the need to stand out. That is why gimmickry abounds all over the dial. Layered, animated typography, for example, has become one way to communicate a message when a viewer's mute button is pressed. Other commercials heap on animation, celebrity spokespersons, experimental music, and choppy, MTV-style editing to look "cutting edge."

It takes more than technique to appeal to the average consumer, who has seen it all a thousand times before. Many creative directors agree that the best campaigns instead touch people on an emotional level, tap into their core needs and desires and sometimes even enhance a person's enjoyment in a product. Wieden & Kennedy's Nike work is continually

recognized for combining all of those ingredients. The campaign has in effect elevated athleticism to the point where sweating is glamorous—even more so when you're wearing the Nike swoosh.

The four creative directors who judged this Casebook were not looking for dazzling camera work or trendy typography. Instead, they were searching for more intangible elements: emotional appeal, relevance, staying power, and a compelling selling point. While not many words were exchanged during the judging process, the judges did occasionally utter a few adjectives, such as, "fresh," "honest," and "real," that revealed volumes about the work they liked.

These down-to-earth qualities scored well because these campaigns were launched in the early '90s, a time when the country was gripped by a recession. Cost-conscious consumers needed many compelling reasons to buy a brand-name product instead of its store-brand counterpart. People responded to advertising that speaks directly to them and addresses their needs. They wanted information, not just entertainment.

Many campaigns in this Casebook wisely seized their products' perceived authenticities and made the most of them. In the late 1980s, Goldsmith/Jeffrey leveraged Everlast's gritty boxing heritage in ads for Everlast Activewear that celebrated macho athleticism while sneering at the trendy and fashion-conscious. The

campaign continues to have relevance in the less-pretentious 1990s, as a 1991 draft of the campaign was chosen by judges. Similarly, Wrangler has long been recognized as an official sponsor of the Professional Rodeo Cowboy Association for over 45 years. The Martin Agency ad campaign shown here cleverly emphasizes this connection by shooting from the point of view of rodeo stars on top of their bucking bulls.

Using real people as company spokespersons also lends a certain authenticity to a product. Frank Perdue and Dave Thomas, for example, have a down-home folksiness that makes people believe their chickens and burgers are as good as they claim they are. Fallon McElligott recognized that Booker Noe, Jim Beam Brand's committed master distiller, was the personification of the premium Booker's Bourbon, so they put him front and center in the newspaper campaign in this book. "The man has bourbon running through his veins," says copywriter Mike Lescarbeau.

Of course, casting ordinary people in commercials is nothing new. But when non-actors are directed with sensitivity, there can be poignant, powerful results. In BBDO/Los Angeles' PowerBook campaign, various people demonstrate how they use their computers to empower themselves. In one commercial, an elderly man who has lived a tough life talks about how he is writing it all down, "where my grandchildren can use it." Streetsmart Advertising also

cast actual homeless people to sing the song "New York, New York" in a wrenching PSA for New York City's Coalition for the Homeless. Art director Leslie Sweet explains that focusing on individuals this way helps to put a human face on homelessness. It also makes the problem hard to ignore.

Campaigns addressing the everyday problems of ordinary people continually cropped up throughout this Casebook, albeit about less serious topics than homelessness. Lee Jeans is positioned by Fallon McElligott as "the brand that fits" by showing the humorous lengths people will go to to struggle into their jeans. Fallon's Windsor Canadian whiskey print campaign also shows how the product is a reward for putting up with everyday hassles, such as waiting in long lines or getting stuck in closing subway car doors.

For younger consumers, advertising imitates life only when it eschews many of its own traditional trappings. "It's anti-advertising," explains Valentine-Radford art director Mary McPhail, describing a Boulevard Beer campaign that makes the company appear as though it couldn't care less if it didn't sell a drop. Headlines in print ads shrug indifferently: "Drink it before someone else does." The same irreverent attitude is found in a Teva Sandals campaign created by Stein Robaire Helm, Los Angeles, in which young men are shown splashing in the surf. Headlines read: "When you die, they'll put you in a shiny suit. As if death didn't suck enough already." That same flippant

attitude ripples through the entire marketing concept of Wise Guise, Inc., a shirt manufacturer started by a former Milwaukee adman. He called his loud, tacky shirts Boy Is That An Ugly Shirt, and its ad campaign by Hoffman York & Compton boasts: "We're looking for people to lose their lunch."

Ironically, some of the best work in this book was the least expensive to make. The work Mad Dogs & Englishmen created for the Village Voice, Tiny Mythic Theatre Company, and the Creative Register was continually praised for being "fresh." What judges didn't know is that many of them cost less than $100 to produce. "It doesn't cost a lot to write a good ad," explains creative director Nick Cohen in his inimitable understated fashion. This sentiment is echoed by Leslie Sweet, a Casebook judge who art-directed two public service campaigns in the book. She says she is tired of hearing creatives complain that they cannot do good advertising on a shoestring. She responds: "Sometimes when you have the least money, you do the best work. It's all about having an idea." As the 39 campaigns in this Casebook will prove, that idea must be suffused with emotion, realism, authenticity, irreverence, and entertainment value. How's that for starters?

—*Joyce Rutter Kaye*

Joyce Rutter Kaye

Joyce Rutter Kaye is managing editor of U&lc, the quarterly international journal of typography and graphic design published by International Typeface Corp. (ITC). Recently, she edited the quarterly Art Directors Club Newsletter for the 75 year-old professional association, and wrote the "Corporate Communications" column for Desktop Communications, a bimonthly magazine published by International Desktop Communications, New York. During 1991-1992, she also acted as advisor to Canvas, the student-run college newspaper of the School of Visual Arts, New York.

Before joining ITC in May 1991, Kaye was a reporter for three years for Advertising Age's monthly magazine, Creativity, where she wrote and edited articles on print advertising, television commercial direction, graphic design, music, and photography. Her articles have appeared in PRINT, How, Idea, Pittsburgh, and the Indianapolis Star Magazine. In 1985, Kaye received a BS degree in magazine journalism from the S.I. Newhouse School of Public Communications of Syracuse University.

Clem McCarthy

Clem McCarthy is executive vice president-associate creative director of Ammirati & Puris, New York, where he has worked on BMW, UPS, Aetna, Waterford and Stanley since 1987. Previous to that, McCarthy worked in his native San Francisco for six years as associate creative director at Hal Riney Partners and later as president of the San Francisco office of BBDO. In 1975, McCarthy joined his present agency as its first creative when it was a fledgling startup. Since then, the agency has grown considerably, to $400 million in billings. In the early days of his career as an art director, McCarthy worked at Ayer, Young & Rubicam and Wells, Rich, Greene. Over the years he has won numerous awards, including Clios, Gold awards from the Art Directors Club and the One Show, and a Lion at the International Advertising Film Festival at Cannes. He is a graduate of Pratt Institute.

Craig Simpson

Craig Simpson is a freelance copywriter currently living in New York. In addition to freelancing at various agencies, he runs a creative consultancy with his art director partner Patrick Milani. Their client list includes Hearst's Town & Country magazine and Look Music, a music production company. From 1990 to 1994, Simpson worked at Kirshenbaum & Bond, New York, where he held the title of associate creative director. His campaigns at K&B include "Your feet won't believe their eyes" for Thom McAnn shoes; "A new breed of broker" for Quick & Reilly Brokerage and "Wake us when it's over" for Charivari fashion stores. Simpson's work has been recognized by Communication Arts, The One Show, and Archive. A native of Portland, Oregon, Simpson graduated from the University of Oregon in 1989 with a BA degree in Journalism.

Leslie Sweet

Leslie Sweet is a New York-based freelance creative director. In the early 1990s, she was vice president-senior art director at McElligott, Wright, Morrison, White in Minneapolis, working on Easy Spirit and Memorial Blood Center. In 1992, Sweet returned to her home base in New York to work at various agencies. During this time, she teamed up with art director Peter Cohen to create pro bono work for the Coalition for the Homeless under the name of Streetsmart Advertising. One commercial in the campaign, "New York, New York," won an Emmy and swept all major advertising awards shows in 1993, including the One Show, the Art Directors Club Awards, the D&AD and the International Advertising Film Festival at Cannes. In addition, the work was selected to appear in this Casebook, along with her television commercials for Memorial Blood Center. From 1988 to 1991, Sweet was vice president-senior art director at Levine, Huntley, Vick & Beaver, New York, working on Dreyfus Corp., Citizen watches, Frito-Lay, Ray-Ban and Dunn & Bradstreet Software Services. Before that, she worked as an art director at the New York offices of Chiat/Day and McCann-Erickson. Sweet, who teaches advertising at the School of Visual Arts, graduated from SUNY/Buffalo in 1980 with a BS degree in advertising.

Bob Tabor

Bob Tabor is senior vice president-group creative director at Bates USA, New York, where he has worked on M&M/Mars, Campbell's Soup, CBS Broadcast Group, Thomas' English Muffins and Arby's since 1985. Tabor has had a long and illustrious career as an art director on Madison Avenue. Fresh out of the School of Visual Arts in 1966, he was hired as an art director at Doyle Dane Bernbach, an agency considered to be one of the leading creative shops during advertising's golden years, working there for five years on Parker Pens, Cool-Ray sunglasses, Quaker Oats and Burlington-Cameo. From 1978 to 1982, he was senior vice president-group creative head at Wells, Rich, Greene, on campaigns for Safeguard Soap and Alka Seltzer. Before joining his present agency, Tabor was senior vice president-creative director at Foote Cone & Belding, creating campaigns for Fritos Corn Chips, Grandma's Cookies and Clairol Essence shampoos. He holds over 50 advertising awards, including Clios and Gold medals from the Art Directors Club.

Clients/Products

Agencies

Art Directors
Creative Directors
Designers/Copywriters

Alexander, Joe **76**
Ammirati, Ralph **90**
Angelo, David **77**
Auslander, Shalom **42, 63**
Barrie, Bob **10, 94**
Bassett, Steve **74**
Berger, David **30, 90**
Bildsten, Bruce **28, 94**
Brahl, Gary **92**
Brihn, Bob **48, 80**
Burnham, Pat **10, 39, 48,
58, 80, 94**
Burns, Scott **66**
Cable, Kim **46**
Cockrell, Bob **20**
Cohen, Nick **42, 63, 84**
Cohen, Peter **32**
Crandall, Court **54**
Dolbinski, Steve **74**
Elwood, Darren **88**
Fazende, Michael **67, 72**
Feuerman, Kerry **76**
Frankel, Clark **15**
Fuller, Mark **70, 76**
Genkinger, Kim **38**
Gier, George **24**
Goldsmith, Gary **86**
Goldstein, Larry **90**
Gomes, Tony **18**
Gordon, Mitch **24**
Griak, Susan **58**
Hampton, Michael **15**
Hanft, Phil **39, 80**
Hanson, Dean **28, 39**
Heller, Amy **42**
Henderson, Dick **38**
Hughes, David **88**
Hutchinson, Nan **90**
Jenkins, David **24**
Johnson, Curt **90**
Jordan, Tom **36, 51**
Ketchum, Greg **20**
Lescarbeau, Mike **48, 58,
67, 72**
Lichtenheld, Tom **60**
Lowe, Guy **46**
Lutz, Dan **92**

Mahoney, John **70**
Marco, Harvey **16**
McKinney, Raymond **52**
McPhail, Mary **92**
Meagher, Bob **74**
Mills, Russlyn **90**
Montague, Ty **42, 84, 86**
Morrison, John **56, 66**
Nelson, Tom **30, 90**
O'Donoghue, Kevin **12**
Olsen, Jarl **10**
Paddock, Jim **46**
Parenio, Sue **15**
Paulini, Barb **36**
Redfern, Peggy **38**
Reich, Mikal **42, 63**
Rhode, Jean **56**
Rockwood, Scott **88**
Rohan, Courtney **42**
Rollins, Gretchen **12**
Scarpelli, Bob **24**
Schwab, Bill **18**
Seisser, Tod **30, 90**
Smith, David **16**
Sorah, Cliff **52, 74**
Souder, Kirk **54**
Spencer, Paul **77**
St. James, Lee **92**
Staffen, John **77**
Stingley, John **60**
Strickland, Carolyn **38**
Sweet, Leslie **32, 56**
Treleven, Todd **50**
Vigon, Jay **12**
Wall, Chris **20**
Wayner, Taras **42, 63**
Westbrook, Bill **70**
Westre, Susan **20**
Wheaton, Mike **50**
Wojdyla, David **30, 90**

Photographers
Illustrators

Arsenault, Dan **88**
Baraban, Joe **77**
Berg, Ron **92**
Conroy, James **46**
Endress, John Paul **15**
Furman, Michael **76**
Gordon, Mitch **24**
Hanauer, Mark **54**
Hellerstein, Steve **86**
Huber, Vic **94**
Jordano, Dave **60**
Kazama, Mitsuo **36**
Lake Michigan Federation **24**
Lamb & Hall **77, 90**
Lampi, Joe **48, 80**
Lanker, Brian **74**
Michienzi, Shawn **94**
Morrill, Dan **24**
Panoramic Images **36**
Perman, Craig **58**
Peterson, Kerry **10, 58**
Reens, Richard **72**
Rubin, Ian **42**
Schneider, Tom **24**
Scott, Mark **74**
Shedd Aquarium **24**
Slavin, Neal **77**
Straube, Werner **24**
Sylvestro, Tony **70**
Wisconsin Sierra Club **24**
Yamashita, Koji **36**

Producers/Directors
Production Companies

Appel, Michael **66**
Belsey, Laura **32**
Brink, Judy **67, 80**
Cohen, Peter **32**
Coppos Films **12, 39, 66, 77**
Coppos, Mark **39, 66**
George, Bill **28**
Herrmann, Eric **77**
Industrial Light & Magic **28**
Kaye, Tony **56**
Kaye, Tony, Films **56**
League of Bald-Headed Men,
The **88**
Levine, Rick, Productions **30**
Limelight Productions **77**
Lloyd, John **77**
Loving, Char **28**
Massey, John **30**
McWalters, Jack **30**
Park Village Productions **67**
PYTKA **20**
Pytka, Joe **20**
RSA/New York **16, 18**
Scott, Jake **16, 18**
Shriber, Bob **16, 18**
Sweet, Leslie **32**
Thomas, Brent **77**
Van Merkensteijn,
Elizabeth **12**
White, Chel **56**
White, Chel, Films **56**
Woodburn, Roger **67**
Young & Co. **80**
Young, Eric **80**

At first, this Hush Puppies for Kids trade ad from Fallon McElligott could be mistaken for one for Tide laundry detergent. The difference here is that the ad is selling washable shoes, not cleaning power. It's a classic example of selling the sizzle, not the steak.

Wolverine gave the nod to this offbeat approach to launch its juvenile Hush Puppies line because the mud-covered shoes clearly demonstrated the product's key attributes—and because subsequent executions in the campaign promised to show the shoes unscathed, according to art director Bob Barrie. "We wanted the visual to carry the power of the ad," he says. The campaign was aimed at children's shoe buyers and ran in issues of the trade magazine Footwear News, where Barrie was certain it would stand out among "page after page of perfect, pristine shoes."

When creating the campaign, Barrie and copywriter Jarl Olsen came up with the visual, then devised a number of headlines to go with it. Here are several of their rejected headlines for this ad: "Don't worry, they're suede"; "Our shoes have never looked better"; and "The shoes will wash off. The socks, however, are ruined." Body copy has a touch of subversive humor, as well, reading: "If a kid gets these specially treated suede and canvas shoes dirty, you can throw them right in the washer. The shoes, that is."

The team considered several alternative concepts

Our new washable shoes.
(They're under there, somewhere.)

If a kid gets these specially treated suede and canvas shoes dirty, you can throw them right in the washer. The shoes, that is. In five durable styles for spring and fall.

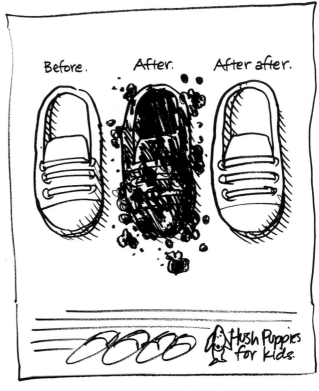

before deciding to pitch mud-covered shoes, an idea which ultimately scored points for working well in a black-and-white format. One rejected ad showed one dirty shoe between two clean ones with the headline, "Before. After. After After." In another, kids' shoes tumbled in a dryer, with the message: "Introducing washable kids' shoes. (Display case optional.)"

Client: Hush Puppies
Agency: Fallon McElligott, Minneapolis, MN
Art director: Bob Barrie
Copywriter: Jarl Olsen
Creative director: Pat Burnham
Photographer: Kerry Peterson

The socks were ruined.
Have you ever seen such a beautiful pair of kids shoes?
This little boy didn't get spanked for ruining his shoes; He got spanked for ruining his socks.
After this photograph was taken, we returned the shoes to the store.
Our shoes have never looked better.
On Sunday, he'll wear these shoes to church.
The shoes will wash off. The socks, however, are ruined.
Our new washable shoes. (They're under there, somewhere.)
Don't worry, they're suede.

Heads for dirty shoes.

Top: initial sketches explored for the campaign; left: a list of headlines Barrie and Olsen brainstormed for final ad.

The marketing directives for this 60-second AT&T Communications commercial were as complex as making a third-party call to Rangoon. The communications giant needed to raise awareness of its long-distance access code (10-ATT-0), which allows travelers to make calls using AT&T services. The commercial not only had to explain how and when to use the access code, it had to work silently, since it would be breaking on in-flight screens, where many passengers would view it without wearing their headphones.

The creative team at Young & Rubicam decided that a stylish, graphic rebus-like approach would do the trick. "Businessman," directed by Mark Coppos of Coppos Films, cleanly weaves spare graphics, typography, and sound effects together to tell a story: A dapper 1940s-style businessman is traveling on the road and decides to call the office. He picks up a pay phone receiver and suddenly remembers that if he doesn't use his access code he may be overcharged by another company. The commercial was aimed at frequent domestic business travelers and appeared on airlines and on network sports programs.

According to copywriter Kevin O'Donoghue, he and art director Gretchen Rollins wanted to create an updated, iconoclastic version of the traveling businessman to add sparkle to a fairly straightforward story. "We wanted to get the message out in a way that was fun," explains Rollins. Type was crucial in the mix. For this they tapped type designer Jay Vigon, who is well known for his broadcast work. Titles set in Futura and other, more expressive typefaces playfully interact with other visual elements in the frames. In one portion of the commercial, for example, the traveler hears a "strange noise" instead of AT&T's familiar "bong" sound when he picks up the receiver. To illustrate this, the word "strange" wavers eerily onscreen like a title from a B horror film. Other titles were improvised during the shoot: When the man decides to call the office, Rollins typed out the word "office" on a "nasty old typewriter," she says, and the word was backed by the sound of an old Royal.

Research showed an increase in awareness of the access code from 40 per cent in January 1991 to 79 per cent at the end of 1992. In 1993, awareness fluctuated with media spending, reaching a high of 70 per cent. In addition, the spot won a gold Effie award for effectiveness in advertising.

The idea for the commercial ironically came from an AT&T spot for a humbler medium devoid of visual cues: radio. In that commercial, the same message was conveyed through a voiceover enhanced with sound effects. It was written by O'Donoghue, who is "fascinated" with the medium. "Most people think of radio as being purely audio," he says. "But I think it truly is one of the most visual outlets. Think of 'War of the Worlds.' Radio is really the theater of the mind."

Storyboards were greatly improvised during the commercial shoot.

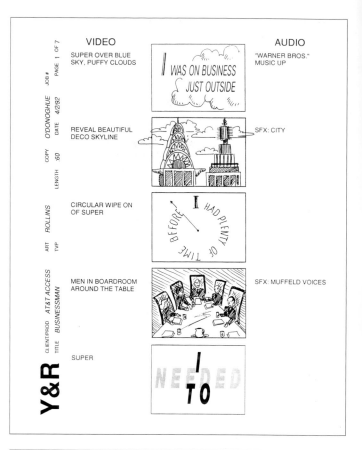

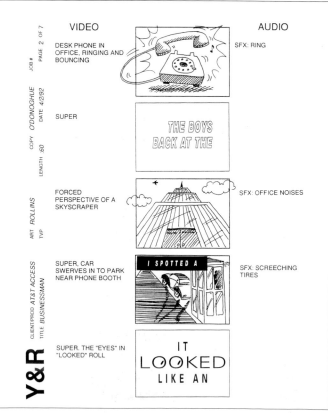

Type designer Jay Vigon's typographic interpretations of the storyboards added impact and an element of fun.

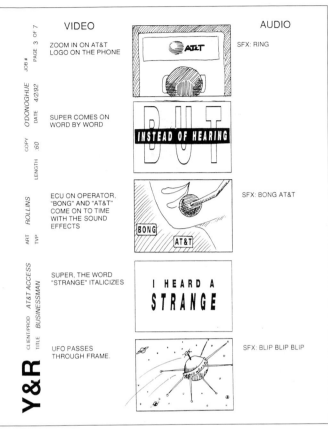

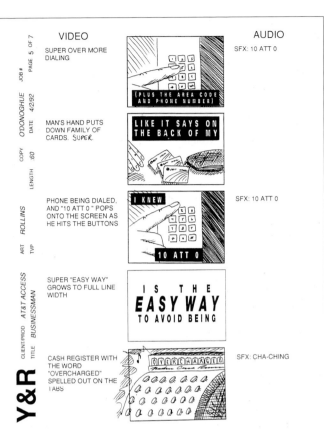

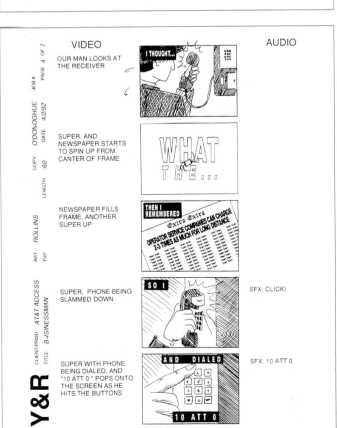

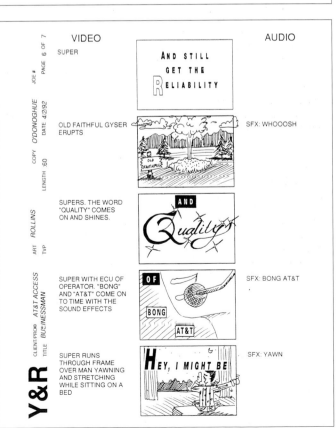

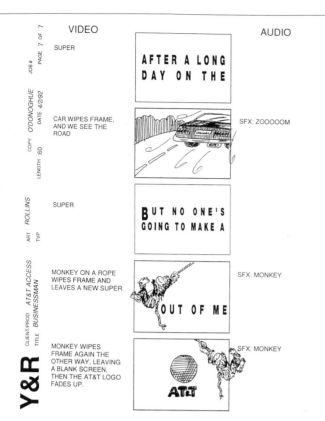

Client: AT&T Communications
Agency: Young & Rubicam, New York, NY
Art director: Gretchen Rollins
Copywriter: Kevin O'Donoghue
Agency producer: Elizabeth Van Merkensteijn
Production company: Coppos Films
Director: Mark Coppos
Editor: Dennis Hayes, Stu Eisenberg
Graphic design/titles: Jay Vigon

The commercial was inspired by radio, says copywriter Kevin O'Donoghue, who calls the medium "theater of the mind."

Sugar Free Jell-O

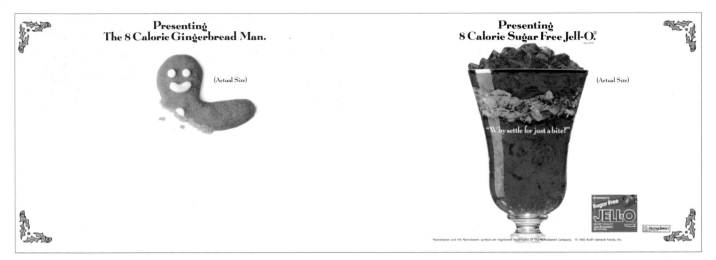

Long before Susan Powter appeared in infomercial-land to tell dieters to stop the insanity and quit starving themselves, Young & Rubicam was doing the same, only without the help of a crew-cut Amazon with a manic mantra. They very quietly demonstrated that for only eight calories, one could eat an entire bowl of Sugar Free Jell-O, versus a crumb of a fattening dessert.

By focusing on Sugar Free Jell-O's unique product attribute (where else will you find a full-sized eight-calorie dessert? Mints don't count), the Y&R creative team helped to revive a product that had strong brand awareness among the target audience of women age 35-plus, but wobbly sales. The campaign needed a sophisticated touch, since the market for the product is quite different from that for sugar-sweetened Jell-O, which is aimed at young families.

According to copywriter Sue Parenio, she and art director Clark Frankel at first considered positioning Sugar Free Jell-O against a wide variety of other eight-calorie snacks—not necessarily sweets. They pitched a commercial showing a late-night snack attack where a refrigerator was searched for something tasty but low-calorie to eat, but yielded nothing more tempting than capers, chutney and ketchup. The message, according to Parenio, was, "Face it, when it's late at night and you want a snack, it's not going to be cornichons."

Kraft liked the idea, but suggested that the creative team focus strictly on desserts. This helped them to dramatize the contrast between foods, especially in print, where they could emphasize scale. In the spreads shown here, they set up tiny portions of desserts—candy bars, ice cream, cookies, against a stark white background with the headline: "Presenting the eight-calorie cookie (ice cream scoop, etc.)." On the right side of the spread, a heaping bowl of Jell-O appears with the headline, "Presenting 8 calorie Sugar Free Jell-O" and the subhead, "Why settle for just a bite?" An accompanying television commercial incorporated shots of each dessert, ending with a woman contentedly eating a bowl of Jell-O while casually flicking away a brownie crumb.

After the campaign's run, research showed a dramatic increase in sales, with 31.9 per cent volume growth, compared to the same Nielsen period the previous year. Post-production testing also revealed high purchase interest: 67 per cent of those tested would "definitely/probably buy" the product. And if those queried do indulge, they can be assured their figures won't wiggle or wobble as a result.

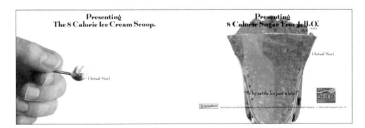

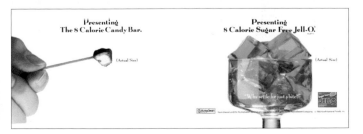

Client: Kraft General Foods
Agency: Young & Rubicam, New York, NY
Art director: Clark Frankel
Copywriter: Sue Parenio
Creative director: Michael Hampton
Photographer: John Paul Endress
Home economist: Maret Price

"How do you improve a brand's image when there is no image to improve?" So mused Ammirati & Puris copywriter David Smith while he and art director Harvey Marco brainstormed on this television commercial for RCA Audio. His answer: "You invent one."

Because RCA was virtually unknown for its audio products among young consumers age 18-34, Thomson Consumer Electronics wanted a commercial for MTV that would position the line as both hip and on the cutting edge of technology. The spot also had to include cameo appearances by Nipper and Chipper, the mascot dogs starring in RCA's two-year old consumer electronics campaign. ("Sunrise," another TV spot in the campaign, also appears in this Casebook.) Although the team had a small ($100,000) budget and a vast number of choices, they felt that by keeping the commercial simple, it would succeed on all fronts.

"Rocker" features a skinny grunge kid with a resemblance to Flea, the eccentric blond bass player of the Red Hot Chili Peppers. Popping a CD in his RCA boom box, he begins to dance manically to the strains of a corny, exaggerated rumba. An announcer deadpans: "Careful. It'll even make your parents' music sound great." Nipper and Chipper, sporting sunglasses, close the spot with the title, "Changing Entertainment. Again." The spot broke in June, 1993. The idea for "Rocker"

materialized from a casual comment Smith made when he and Marco were experimenting with the RCA CD boom box in their office. Impressed with its clarity of sound, Smith said, "I bet even Lawrence Welk sounds great on this." "After that, the commercial really created itself," says Marco.

Several rejected ideas stemmed from a line borrowed from an old campaign by the previous agency: "RCA Audio. It will blow you away." One commercial showed blow-up dolls who inflate, float to the ceiling and finally explode. Another spot featured a gerbil on a wheel in his cage. Suddenly, a stereo begins playing "Born Free." Spotting an open field outside the window, the gerbil musters up the courage to burst through the glass and escape into the great outdoors. The latter idea "never made it into testing," says Marco with a laugh.

Casting for "Rocker" was crucial. The actor had to be ultra-hip, but also be friendly, accessible and able to move to a groove. Although Smith and Marco screened a wide variety of candidates, from body-pierced skinheads to tattooed bikers, "no one was ideal," recalls Marco. (Particularly not the two gentlemen who, when asked to dance, performed a racy burlesque and stripped to their underwear.) Finally, one day before the shoot, a casting director spotted Rick, a musician/magician/actor/filmmaker at the Farmer's Market in Los Angeles, and knew at once that this was the

"rocker" they were seeking.

Response to the commercials has been very favorable from consumers and retailers alike. Service Merchandise requested rights to play the commercial on display televisions in stores, a privilege usually requested by the client. In addition, say Smith and Marco, RCA also toyed with the idea of taking Rick on a national tour to dance in stores and appear with Nipper and Chipper. "I think that idea was dropped," says Marco.

Rocker
30 seconds
(SFX: CD being inserted into player.
Music comes up.)
VO: RCA Audio. Careful, it'll even make your parent's music sound great.

Client: Thomson Consumer Electronics
Agency: Ammirati & Puris, New York, NY
Art director: Harvey Marco
Copywriter: David Smith
Agency producer: Bob Shriber
Production company: RSA/New York
Director: Jake Scott
Editor: Vito DeSario

RCA's solid, respected, apple-pie brand name has for years earned it the largest market share for color televisions. In recent years, however, older consumers who grew up with the brand were not being replaced, as younger people were instead choosing Japanese brands such as Sony and Mitsubishi. Furthermore, RCA needed to expand its visibility beyond standard TV sets to include its other home electronics products, such as VCRs, laser disk players and audio equipment. "RCA had an old, stodgy image. They had to dust it off," says Ammirati & Puris associate creative director Tony Gomes, who wrote "Sunrise," one of two 30-second spots singled out by the Casebook judges from the long-running image campaign created by the agency. ("Rocker," the other spot, is discussed on page 16.)

To breathe life into RCA's image, the agency reintroduced Nipper, the faithful, familiar RCA mascot, to represent the company's steadfast commitment to quality. Chipper, his new sidekick, was added to stand for the company's new generation of electronic products (and also to up the cuteness factor). In this television campaign, Nipper and Chipper team up to demonstrate different qualities of the products by interacting with them.

In "Sunrise," for large-screen TVs (or "home theaters," as they are called), for example, Chipper trots into a room where a potted sunflower droops before the large-screen TV. The dog

paws the button on the remote control, and suddenly the room is bathed in light. As Johnny Nash's hit, "I Can See Clearly Now," plays, the sunflower slowly unbends toward the brilliant light. This tack was used because research had shown that the product was the brightest projection television on the market. The sunflower idea came about during a brainstorming session, says Gomes, when someone commented, "It's so bright, it would probably give you a tan." By using the dogs to interact with the products, two messages come across, adds Gomes. "They have a homespun quality about them, but the televisions are technological marvels as well."

Although the commercials for the luxury product ran during a recession, sales increased in the very large (30" and over) screen category by 68 per cent during the on-air period of October 1991-February 1993. Gomes attributes this to the fact that during the tough economy, people spent their entertainment dollars on products for the home. "Sales of consumer electronics grew during that time," he says.

RCA
Changing Entertainment. Again.

Client: Thomson Consumer Electronics
Agency: Ammirati & Puris, New York, NY
Art director: Bill Schwab
Copywriter: Tony Gomes
Agency producer: Bob Shriber
Production company: RSA/New York
Director: Jake Scott

Sunrise
30 seconds
(SFX: Dog sniffing. Song "I Can See Clearly Now" comes up.)

VO: Presenting the RCA 52" projection screen home theater. It's bigger and brighter than almost anything out there.

Apple Computer's key selling point has always been its ease of use—an attribute the company calls the "Macintosh Advantage." When Microsoft began poaching that territory in the early 1990s by touting its Windows software as the easiest operating system on the market, Apple needed to aggressively reaffirm its position. The company wanted an advertising campaign that would dispel the myths it felt were being spread in the Microsoft ads about the similarity of the two systems.

With this marketing directive in mind, BBDO produced a 1992 campaign theme, "The Hard Way/The Easy Way," showing side-by-side comparisons between the two products. Print ads feature spreads in which one side, titled "The Hard Way," tells of the difficulties in using Windows, while the opposite page points out the advantages of using a Macintosh.

Television commercials feature amusing vignettes of business people frustrated over the confusing technical jargon in Windows' manual, "Getting Started with Windows." Two of those commercials, "Making it Easier" and "Diner," were selected by the Casebook judges. Each portrays Windows as presenting the learning curve from hell. Director Joe Pytka's flair for capturing emotional, realistic performances helped elevate the anxiety level even further. Both commercials ran on network television from November 1992 through August 1993.

"Making it Easier" features two executives hunched over a computer in their cluttered office, trying in vain for hours to print a document from Windows. "If you're printing to the LPT1, try printing to the LPT1-dot-DOS file instead," one of them reads directly from the Windows manual. A female co-worker passes by and asks what they're doing. "Making it easier to use," says one exec. "So we'll be more productive," adds the other. She isn't impressed. "If you're this productive much longer," she replies, "we'll go out of business."

"Diner" shows two different businessmen struggling over their PC notebook computer and the Windows manual at a remote roadside diner, while a gaggle of amused locals take turns taking potshots at the hotshots from the city. When the men lose a file on the system, a waitress passes by and smirks, "You sure you guys know what you're doing?" and begins to guffaw. Several booths away, a yuppie is seen hammering contentedly at his PowerBook. Copywriter Greg Ketchum teamed with art director Bob Cockrell on the spot; "Making it Easier" was created by art director Susan Westre and copywriter Chris Wall, the two creative directors who head the account.

According to Ketchum, the remote setting in "Diner" served to emphasize to laptop users that while their computers may be portable, so are their Windows problems. "We wanted to

Making it Easier
60 seconds
Executive 1: Using the text editor, open the System I-N-I file.
Executive 2: You mean the System "ini" file.
Executive 1: Type the DIR command to see how much space is in…
Executive 2: "C," colon, backslash, windows, backslash, system…
Executive 1: Find the 386…
Woman: Need any help?
Both executives: No.
Executive 1: …the 386 E…
Executive 1: …device command in this example sets up the H-I-M-E-M-dot-SYS device driver…
Executive 2: I did something wrong.
Executive 1: What?
Executive 2: We're back in DOS.
Executive 1: …if you're printing to the LPT1, try printing to the LPT1-dot-DOS file instead…
Executive 2: Whoops!
Executive 1: What?
Executive 2: What did I do?
Executive 1: I don't know. Page 99…
Woman: What are you guys doing? You've been fooling with that thing for three days now.
Executive 2: Making it easier to use.
Executive 1: So we'll be more productive.
Woman: If you're this productive much longer we'll go out of business.
VO: If you want a computer that's easy to use, there's still only one way to go.

The Hard Way/The Easy Way
Client: Apple Computer
Agency: BBDO, Los Angeles, CA
Art directors: Susan Westre ("Making It Easier"), Bob Cockrell ("Diner")
Copywriters: Chris Wall ("Making It Easier"), Greg Ketchum ("Diner")
Creative directors : Chris Wall, Susan Westre
Production company: PYTKA
Director: Joe Pytka

Diner
60 seconds
(SFX: Diner sounds, dishes, radio music.)
Executive 1: Set TEMP equals "C," colon, slash, T-M-P.
Executive 2: "C," colon, slash, T-N-P.
Executive 1: M…T-M-P.
Executive 2: T-M-P, right.
Executive 1: If there's an interrupt conflict with the serial or bus port, then…
Executive 2: If there's an interrupt conflict? What is that?
Diner: You guys aren't from around here, are ya?
Executive 2: Chapter 4, trouble shooting.
Executive 2: Didn't you just do this? You told me you could do this.
Executive 1: Would you help me on this, please?
Executive 2: I'm trying. But, we've been sitting here…I can't make this work. I can't do both…
Executive 1: What happened?
Executive 2: Wait a minute
Executive 1: What?
Executive 2: File not found. It says file not found.
Executive 1: You lost the presentation?
Executive 2: It's here…it's not gone.
Diner: A computer, huh?
Executive 1: Yeah.
Executive 2: Listen. Do you wanna just call the support line? Try it again please.
Waitress: You sure you guys know what you're doing? (Laughs)
VO: If you want a computer that's easy to use, there's still only one way to go.

show that when you're on the road, your technical advisor won't be there down the hall for you," he says, "so you'd better have your DOS manual with you."

PowerBook

"What's on your PowerBook?" asks the commercials for Apple's popular notebook computer. In the three spots chosen for this Casebook, this question is posed to a grandfather, a teacher, and a haiku writer. Their answers reveal less about their computer's RAM and software programs than about the myriad ways they use their PowerBooks to empower themselves. Hence the tagline: "What's on Your PowerBook Is You."

"Teacher" shows a young woman in a darkened schoolroom, writing up class evaluations. It is obvious she is fiercely committed to her role as an educator: "I want to help you do things you didn't know you could do," she says. "Anyone can be a critic. I want to be a teacher."

In the poignant "Grandfather," an elderly man is shown writing his journal on his PowerBook. His face is creased with wisdom and experience. "I've been a soldier and a father," he says. "I have made mistakes...I'm putting it all down where my grandchildren can use it."

On a lighter note, "Haiku Guy" features a young man in a Hawaiian shirt who perches on a beach chair, rattling off the goofy haikus he composes on his PowerBook: "I-am-but-a-piece-of-sand," he says. "Bread-violin-watch it-quag-mire-Power-Book-exclamation.

Grandma-wanted me-to be a lawyer-but no."

By personifying the computer through mini-profiles of its variety of users, this BBDO campaign attempts to show that the computer is somehow a reflection of each user. In a way, they are the Dewar's Profiles of the 1990s. "That's true," agrees creative director/copywriter Chris Wall, who worked on the campaign with creative director/art director Susan Westre. "But the difference here is that the PowerBook is involved in every aspect of your life." The television campaign, consisting of 12 commercials, ran from August through November 1993 on network television. An accompanying print campaign ran in consumer magazines. Although the same question—"What's on Your PowerBook?"—was posed in print, each execution shows two very different PowerBook users from different walks of life to contrast the ways people use their computers. The campaign was targeted to people 18-54 with incomes of $40,000 and more.

BBDO had introduced the PowerBook line in 1991 with a campaign that emphasized its convenience and ease of use. In one spot, for example, Kareem Abdul-Jabbar is squeezed into an airline's coach section, but his hands are comfortable on the PowerBook keyboard. The follow-up effort in 1993 needed to maintain its cachet and build up the brand's personality further, says Wall.

According to Wall, most of

Teacher
60 seconds
(SFX: Music in background)
Teacher: I don't wanna be a critic...I wanna be a builder...I wanna be a doer...I wanna challenge you...I wanna help you do things that you didn't know you could do... Anyone can be a critic...I wanna be a teacher.

the commercials were unscripted and cast with non-actors. They were directed by Joe Pytka, who encourages improvisation on the set. Initially, three or four commercials were scripted, but Pytka and creatives decided to shoot 13 people instead, with some of them shot in just one take. The creative team credits Pytka for the realism of the spots. "He has an eye for the two-, three-, or four-second moment," says Wall. "Sometimes people don't even realize he's shooting." Soon after the campaign broke, Apple received hundreds of letters from people who wanted to be featured in the campaign, from doctors and lawyers to famous entertainers.

Grandfather
30 seconds
(SFX: Background music)
Grandfather: I'm 77 years old...I've been a soldier and a father...I've been to war...I've raised a family...I have made mistakes...I've done things I didn't believe I could do...I'm putting it all down where my grandchildren can use it.

Haiku Guy
30 seconds
(SFX: Ocean waves)
Poet: I'm a haiku poet.
(SFX: Music comes up with ocean waves)
Poet: I-am-but-a-piece-of-sand. Rocks-are-like-big-chunks-of-time. Corporations are...
Poet: You know they just come to me like this.
(SFX: Finger snap)
Poet: Something-I-know-nothing-of...I get 'em down here and then they're here. Bread-violin-watch it-quag-mire-Power-Book-exclamation. Grandma-wanted me-to be a lawyer-but no.

PowerBook
Client: Apple Computer
Agency: BBDO, Los Angeles, CA
Art director: Susan Westre
Copywriter: Chris Wall
Creative directors: Chris Wall, Susan Westre
Production company: PYTKA
Director: Joe Pytka

Chicagoans regard Lake Michigan as being safe to swim in and drink from (after treatment, of course). But if you look beneath the surface, the lake is a veritable liquid landfill of toxic chemicals, according to the Lake Michigan Federation, a local water conservation group. Because of too-lax dumping laws, they say, the Great Lakes are brimming with PCBs, lead, mercury and other chemicals from industry, as well as waste from farms and municipalities. This has poisoned the fish, caused mutated bills in birds, and could contribute to birth defects in humans.

With this pro bono newspaper campaign created by DDB Needham/Chicago, the conservation group wanted to educate readers about the water pollution issue and motivate them to take action. Since the campaign targeted the educated, affluent readers of the suburban Elmhurst Press, a genteel, literary approach was favored over the "shock" tactics often used in environmental campaigns, according to creative director/art director Mitch Gordon, who teamed with copywriter George Gier. "They wanted to establish credibility immediately, because they are not a radical, fly-by-night organization," says Gordon, who feels that preachy, intimidating campaigns are probably more effective in attracting awards for their creators than support for a cause. "People are tired of being told what to do," he contends. "We felt it boiled down to this: Are you the kind of guy or woman who's going

---

EITHER THERE IS AN EXTRAORDINARY AMOUNT OF TOXINS IN THE LAKE, OR FISH HAVE FOUND A WAY TO SMOKE CIGARETTES UNDER WATER.

For years, the Surgeon General has put labels on cigarettes to warn us of the dangers of smoking. Now it may not be too long before the Surgeon General must issue a warning about our water as well. With all the industry around the Great Lakes dumping heavy metals, chemicals and grease in the water, our lakes have become cesspools filled with toxic waste.

Fish have already felt the effects of the pollution. Some have tumors, others can't reproduce and others show deformities.

Birds, mammals and other animals are suffering too. Toxins in the water cause cormorants that nest near Green Bay to be born with crossed bills. These mutated beaks make it impossible for the birds to eat and they slowly starve to death.

More visible deformities are crossed bills as with this young cormorant.

Are we next? There are already signs that what is destroying the wildlife will not stop at the shores of the Great Lakes. Investigating the effects of pollution along the Niagara River, a heavily polluted waterway running into Lake Erie, Dr. Beverly Paigen found that children born to parents living in the area suffered birth defects at a rate three times higher than normal. These defects included: webbed feet, extra toes and kidney abnormalities.

In one of the most disturbing studies, Wayne State University researchers found that children of mothers who ate PCB-contaminated fish from Lake Michigan did not learn as well as other people not exposed to PCBs.

How has this happened? For over a hundred years industry has been allowed to dump hazardous wastes in the Great Lakes with little or no control. The lakes, rivers, and ground water of the Great Lakes basin have become a landfill for hundreds of millions of tons of waste.

Common tern eggs, like this, develop shells so thin the bird never has a chance to hatch.

In addition, pesticide runoff from farms, municipal waste and landfills has contributed to the contamination. In his 1986 book *The Late Great Lakes: An Environmental His-* tory, William Ashworth notes: "At

LAKE TROUT
Toxins in the water collect in the fatty tissue, making fish like this as lethal as cigarettes.

the southern end of Lake Michigan, near Chicago, there is a harbor with a floor that is half PCBs and another in which the bottom sludge is forty percent mud and sixty percent a sort of twentieth-century witch's brew involving PCBs, chromium, zinc, lead, oil and grease, iron and various compounds…"

But what can we do? You don't have to be a senator to make a difference in the Great Lakes. In 1971 the Lake Michigan Federation got the Chicago City Council to ban phosphates in detergents. Then we worked with other environmental organizations to get detergent phosphates banned in Wisconsin, Michigan and Indiana.

Volvox: An algae that is part of the delicate balance in the food chain that is altered by toxins.

The fight to ban phosphates in detergents went on to become one of the big environmental battles of the '70s and this victory is one of the reasons Lake Michigan is looking cleaner today. However, now we have to save the lake from toxic chemicals.

Night Heron

The toxin poisoning can't continue. We have to eliminate them completely from our environment. Reducing the limit industry can legally dump, diluting them or relocating them won't alleviate the problem – no matter what,

they'll always find their way back to our water supply. We must stop dumping them altogether. This is what we call zero discharge, and it is really our only hope. If we act now it is not too late to save Lake Michigan, the other Great Lakes and their waterways. We can make them safe and clean for our children and grandchildren.

It seems an enormous task, but consider the alternatives. We go about living our lives the way we do now. The deformities in wildlife multiply. Our risk of cancer and deformities in children continue to rise.

PERHAPS THE SURGEON GENERAL SHOULD PUT WARNING LABELS ON FISH.

A recent study conducted at the University of Michigan found levels of pesticides in women with breast cancer fifty to sixty times greater than levels in women without breast cancer.

"The findings weren't subtle. They were very dramatic," said Dr. Frank Falk.

Among these pesticides are DDT, BCH and HCB. A veritable alphabet soup of toxins. Also found were high levels of PCBs and PBBs.

Where did these chemicals come from? Manufacturing and agriculture have been using them for generations.

And to this day they are still being dumped into the Great Lakes, or are running off into the lakes in alarming quantities. As they make their way up the food chain they become concentrated in the fatty tissue of fish and other animals, including people.

But there is hope. If we begin cleaning up our waterways now, we can help reduce the risk of our daughters and grand-daughters suffering from these poisons.

The toxic sediment at the bottoms of our lakes, rivers and streams grows. It won't be long before we're living very near five of the largest hazardous waste dumps in the world.

If you want to know what you can do to help, call the Lake Michigan Federation at 1-312-939-0839. We're not only looking for donations, we're looking for help, ideas and commitment.

The LAKE MICHIGAN FEDERATION

59 E. Van Buren St., Suite 2215, Chicago, IL 60605 312·939·0838

The Lake Michigan Federation is a not-for-profit, grassroots environmental organization founded in 1970 to promote citizen action to protect a Great Lake. For the past twenty- *two years the Federation has been working to: improve water quality in the Lake; promote sound plans for shoreline management; and increase Lake appreciation through education.*

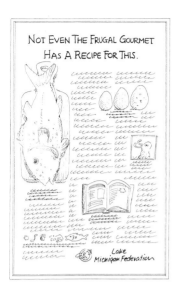
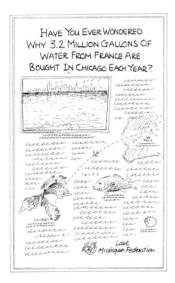
HAVE YOU EVER WONDERED WHY 3.2 MILLION GALLONS OF WATER FROM FRANCE ARE BOUGHT IN CHICAGO EACH YEAR?

The largest freshwater reservoir in the world, The Great Lakes, puts one-fifth of the earth's drinkable water at our doorstep.

They are everywhere, hundreds of thousands of little trendy bottles imported all the way from France. Today people will pay an outrageous price for something we once considered an almost unlimited commodity — water.

There's a reason people are buying a lot of bottled water: they're afraid of the toxins and impurities in their ordinary tap water. Though our tap water is filtered to make drinkable, we can't be sure how pure it really is. So their fears are not unfounded. Toxic discharge into the Great Lakes has become so widespread and so concentrated you no longer need sophisticated water testing equipment to see the damage.

Common tern eggs, like this, develop shells too thin the bird never has a chance to hatch.

Fish, birds and wildlife near the lakes and rivers that run into them are suffering from deformities, tumors, and are having trouble reproducing.

And there's evidence that these toxic manifestations are showing up in people. For example, people who eat just one lake trout in the course of their lifetime increase their risk of cancer by ten times. And children born to parents living in highly polluted areas were found to have birth defects at three times the normal rate.

Puccoon

How has this happened? For over a hundred years industry has been allowed to dump hazardous wastes in the Great Lakes with little or no legislation governing them. The lakes, rivers, and ground water of the Great Lakes basin became a veritable landfill for hundreds of thousands of tons of waste. In addition pesticide runoff from farms, municipal waste and landfills have all contributed to the contamination. In

his 1986 book, *The Late Great Lakes: An Environmental History,* William Ashworth notes: "At the southern end of Lake Michigan, near Chicago, there is a harbor with a floor that is half PCBs and another in which the bottom sludge is 40 percent mud and 60 percent a sort of twentieth-century witch's brew involving PCBs, chromium, zinc, lead, oil and grease, iron and various compounds…"

Not all the toxic waste in the Great Lakes comes from industry, agriculture or landfill leaching. Another big source of toxins is the everyday products we use to clean our homes and cars. Cleansers, rug shampoos, degreasers, foaming agents are just a handful of the products that go down the drain and into our water. Additionally, lawn care products and fertilizers add a lot to the pollution. That doesn't mean we can't turn back the tide of destruction. To do this we have to stop using our lakes as liquid landfills. Industry has to find ways of manufacturing that won't pollute. We have to convince people to stop using hazardous household products that get flushed into our water. Farmers need help in finding alternative ways of farming that don't require mass dumpings of chemical pesticides and fertilizers.

How can one person make a difference? Well, you don't have to be a senator to help clean up the Great Lakes. In

Bittern

No, this is not an ad for bottled water importers.

1970 a group of women in Buffalo banded together and formed "Housewives to End Pollution." They mounted a campaign to force grocery stores to list the phosphate content of detergent right on store shelves. Determined to use whatever tactics necessary, their word spread. More and more groups like theirs formed. The fight to ban phosphates in detergents became one of the big environmental battles of the '70s. Their victory is one of the reasons we still have the Great Lakes to try and save 20 years later.

Perhaps the first thing we can all do to make a difference in the lakes starts right at home. Use safe alternatives, like baking soda, to cleansers, recycle used motor oil, and use soap and water whenever possible instead of harsh chemicals.

If we don't begin the cleanup now, we must consider the alternatives: We go about living our lives the way we do now. The deformities in wildlife multiply. Our risks of cancer and deformities in children continue to rise. The toxic sediment at the bottom of our lakes, rivers and streams grows. It won't be long before we're living very near five of the largest hazardous dumps in the world.

Legally, millions of tons of toxins are poured into the lakes each year from outlets like this.

Water is elemental to life and fourteen million people depend on Lake Michigan for drinking water.

If you want to help, now's the time. We not only need donations, we need your ideas and your commitment. Call us at 312-939-0838 and help reverse the tide.

LAKE MICHIGAN FEDERATION

59 E. Van Buren St., Suite 2215, Chicago, IL 60605 312·939·0838

The Lake Michigan Federation is a not-for-profit, grassroots environmental organization founded in 1970 to promote citizen action to protect a Great Lake. For the past twenty- *two years the Federation has been working to: improve water quality in the Lake; promote sound plans for shoreline management; and increase Lake appreciation through education.*

to listen to someone yell at you at the top of their lungs, or sit down and quietly have a conversation about the pros and cons of the issue?'"

The campaign uses wry humor in headlines to draw readers into an editorial-style layout with article-length copy illustrated with mezzotints of healthy and mutated flora and fauna. One ad whose head reads, "Either there is an extraordinary amount of toxins in the lake, or fish have found a way to smoke cigarettes underwater," describes how the concentration of toxins in the fatty tissue of fish makes them as "lethal as cigarettes," then explains the implications of diseased fish on the entire food chain. The overall style is reminiscent of a late-1980s award-winning campaign for The Nature Company by Goodby, Berlin Silverstein, which used an editorial style to lure readers into reading about the store's wares.

Although the message in the Lake Federation's campaign is grim, copy does offer hope that it is possible to reverse the tide, promising, "If we begin cleaning up our waterways now, we can help reduce the risk of our daughters and granddaughters suffering from these poisons." Or as Gordon puts it, "The lake does have all these things in it, but it's not the Hudson River."

THIS ISN'T SOMETHING OUT OF JULES VERNE, IT'S A FISH OUT OF LAKE MICHIGAN.

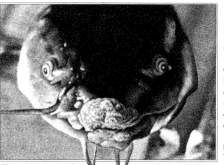

The signs of toxic poisoning are showing up in fish in the form of lesions, tumors, and cancer.

When a Canadian newspaper announced it was sponsoring a fishing contest on Lake Ontario, sportfishermen turned out in droves. After a full day out on the lake the contestants brought in their catch of the day and a winner was determined. But that day the biggest fish didn't win. Shortly after the winner was announced, the judge determined that it could not possibly have been caught in Lake Ontario — it wasn't contaminated enough.

Although you can't see it, the toxics that contaminated Lake Ontario are contaminating Lake Michigan and the other Great Lakes. They have become liquid landfills for toxic wastes the likes the world has never seen. PCBs, chromium, lead, mercury, DDT, dioxin; you name it, the lakes have it. And every day the pollution continues. Industry continues to dump in tons of toxics, runoff from farms and municipalities add more, and airborne toxics contribute up to half the amount in Lake Michigan alone.

Many stages of the food chain, like this tadpole, are affected by toxins.

Where does it all go? Most of it settles on the bottom creating a hazardous muck that would make drinking motor oil seem safe. But it doesn't just sit there. Along comes a small organism like a snail that absorbs it in its system. Then a fish swims along and eats a few snails. The concentration of toxics grows. Then a bigger fish eats a few dozen smaller fish and so on. By the time we work up the food chain the concentration of hazardous wastes in their bodies increases anywhere from ten thousand to a million times greater than levels found in the water.

A Caspian Tern embryo with a crossed bill preserved for further research.

This process is called biomagnification, and it is taking its toll at the top of the food chain—us. The effects of toxic wastes have begun to show up in people living in the Great Lakes region. Birth defects, low birth weights,

stress sensitivity and slow growth were found in babies whose mothers ate at least one fish weekly with a high accumulation of PCBs. Sadly, once some of these toxics get into the DNA of humans, they may be passed on for generations to come. A genealogical nightmare for families of the region.

For over a hundred years industry has been dumping hazardous wastes in the Great Lakes with little or no legislation governing them, making the Great Lakes basin a landfill for tons of waste. Pesticide runoff from farms, municipal waste and landfills have all contributed to the contamination.

A big source of toxins is the everyday products we use to clean up our homes and our cars. Cleansers, rug shampoos, degreasers and foaming agents are just a few of the products that go down the drain and into our water.

Eggs from shore birds often develop shells so thin they never get a chance to hatch.

In his 1986 book, *The Late Great Lakes: An Environmental History,* William Ashworth notes: "At the southern end of Lake Michigan, near Chicago, there is a harbor with a floor that is half PCBs and another in which the bottom sludge is forty percent mud and sixty percent a sort of twentieth-century witch's brew

involving PCBs, chromium, zinc, lead, oil and grease, iron and various compounds…"

To clean up the Great Lakes will cost billions. But cleanup can't begin until we stop *Bufflehead* the poisoning. That means zero discharge of all hazardous chemicals that concentrate in the food chains.

How can we possibly hope for zero discharge? It starts with you. The movement toward cleaning up our environment has just begun. Pressure from the public has been instrumental in getting rid of foam packaging in fast food restaurants and creating an entire new line of environmentally safe consumer products.

IF WATER CATCHES ON FIRE WHAT DO YOU PUT IT OUT WITH?

In 1971, the residents near the Niagara River were asking themselves that very question. Pollutants such as grease, oil and sludge being dumped into the river became a soupy quagmire of highly flammable scum.

One day, when a spark from a worker's acetylene torch hit the river, it ignited, and flames raged twenty feet high. The fire quickly spread down the river and incinerated bridges and scorched the banks.

It prompted city officials to put up signs near the river warning people of the potential fire hazard.

Twenty years later the pollution that plugged up the river and created a fire hazard has been drastically reduced. But therein lies the problem we are faced with today: toxins. You see, since the Great Lakes and their rivers look much better than they have in the past, people seem to think pollution is no longer a threat.

However, what they can't see, the poisonous toxic waste that's dumped into them each day, threatens to affect all of us in a much more severe way. That's what the Lake Michigan Federation aims to clean up. And it all starts with you.

Perhaps the first thing we can all do to make a real difference in the lakes starts right in our homes. For instance, use safe alternatives, like baking soda, to harsh cleansers, recycle used motor oil, and use soap and water whenever possible instead of harsh chemicals. Help us start the cleanup. Call us at 312-939-0838. Donations are needed, but so are your ideas and commitment.

The LAKE MICHIGAN FEDERATION

59 E. Van Buren St., Suite 2215, Chicago, IL 60605 312·939·0838

The Lake Michigan Federation is a not-for-profit, grassroots environmental organization founded in 1970 to promote citizen action to protect a Great Lake. For the past twenty- *two years the Federation has been working to: improve water quality in the Lake; promote sound plans for shoreline management; and increase Lake appreciation through education.*

NOT EVEN THE FRUGAL GOURMET HAS A RECIPE FOR THIS.

There's no safe way to eat this fish. Stored inside its flesh and fatty tissues are concentrations of hazardous wastes thousands of times higher than what the EPA considers safe.

In fact, eating just one trout from Lake Michigan in your lifetime will increase your chances of getting cancer tenfold. Eating just eleven lake trout in your lifetime will better your chances of cancer by 100 times.

But this is not a fish story. What's happening to the aquatic life in

BROOK TROUT
You can dice it and slice it but it's still going to increase your chances of getting cancer.

the Great Lakes is only the beginning.

Birds, mammals and other wildlife are suffering too. Toxics in the water already cause some cormorants to be born with mutated bills. With their crossed beaks they can't eat and slowly starve to death. Turtles have been found with large tumors and, ironically, some mink have been unable to reproduce. So where does this leave us? Well, we're tops on the food chain and there are already signs that the toxics in the water are getting to us. A recent study conducted in Michigan showed that children born to mothers who consumed fish were smaller and did not develop as well as children of women who never ate these contaminated fish.

Sand Cherry

How has this happened? For over a hundred years industry has been allowed to dump hazardous wastes in the Great Lakes with little or no legislation governing them. The lakes, rivers, and ground water of the Great Lakes basin became a

veritable landfill for hundreds of thousands of tons of waste.

In his 1986 book, *The Late Great Lakes: An Environmental History*, William Ashworth notes: "At the Southern end of Lake Michigan, near Chicago, there is a harbor with a floor that is half PCBs and another in which the bottom sludge is 40 percent mud and 60 percent a sort of twentieth-century witch's brew involving PCBs, chromium, zinc, lead, oil and grease, iron and various compounds…"

Early stages of the food chain, like the snail, are affected.

Not all the toxic waste in the Great Lakes comes from industry. Pesticide runoff from farms, municipal waste and landfills all add to the problem. For example, some of the products we use to clean our homes and our cars are among the most toxic of all waste being dumped into the water. Household cleaners, rug shampoo, and old motor oil are just some of the chemicals that go right down the drain into our water.

However, the pollution doesn't just sit there on the lake floor. Along comes a small organism like a snail that has no choice but to absorb it in its system. Then a fish swims along and eats a few snails. The concentration of toxics grows. Then a bigger fish eats a few dozen smaller fish and so on. By the time we work up the food chain to sportfish like lake trout, large birds or mammals that live near the shores, the concentration of hazardous wastes in their bodies increases anywhere from ten thousand to a million

Double-crested Cormorant, Tern and Osprey eggs often never get a chance to hatch because of thin shells

times greater than levels found in the water. But what can we do? You don't have to be a senator to make a difference in the Great Lakes. In 1970 a group of women in Buffalo banded together and formed "Housewives to End Pollution." They mounted a campaign to force grocery stores to list the phosphate content of detergent right on store shelves. Determined to use whatever tactics necessary, their word spread. More and more groups like theirs formed. The fight to ban phosphates in detergents became one of the big environmental battles of the '70s and their victory is one of the reasons we still have the Great Lakes to try and save 20 years later. But perhaps the best thing we can do to clean up our lakes starts right at home. Use safe alternatives to harsh chemicals, like baking soda, recycle your motor oil every change, and clean with ordinary soap and water.

Deformed from toxins, this young cormorant can't catch fish and will slowly starve to death.

Our lakes and waterways are really at a critical point in their history. If we begin to turn back the generations of misuse now we can help them to heal themselves. But to do this we must stop dumping immediately. No amount of toxic wastes that accumulate in the food chain can be tolerated.

If you want to help, call us at 312-939-0838. (If you like, we even have a list of safe alternative household cleansers that will clean your house without polluting the water.) Call today, and help make the water safe for the fish and the fish safe for us.

(The) LAKE MICHIGAN FEDERATION
59 E. Van Buren St., Suite 2215, Chicago, IL 60605 312·939·0838

The Lake Michigan Federation is a not-for-profit, grassroots environmental organization founded in 1970 to promote citizen action to protect a Great Lake. For the past twenty-two years the Federation has been working to: improve water quality in the Lake; promote sound plans for shoreline management; and increase Lake appreciation through education.

THIS ISN'T SOMETHING OUT OF JULES VERNE, IT'S A TROUT OUT OF LAKE MICHIGAN.

EITHER THERE IS AN EXTRAORDINARY AMOUNT OF TOXICS IN THE WATER, OR FISH HAVE FOUND A WAY TO SMOKE CIGARRETTES UNDER WATER.

Above: early sketches of final layouts.

Client: Lake Michigan Federation
Agency: DDB Needham, Chicago, IL
Art director: Mitch Gordon
Copywriter: George Gier
Creative directors: Bob Scarpelli, David Jenkins
Photographers: Tom Schneider, Werner Straube, Shedd Aquarium, Dan Morrill, Wisconsin Sierra Club, Lake Michigan Federation, Mitch Gordon
Retoucher: Jim Menz

Timex had two directives for the advertising campaign launching its new line of glow-in-the-dark IndiGlo watches. The television commercial had to both demonstrate the watches' improved luminescent technology, and show a humorous "torture test," to prove it could "take a licking and keep on ticking." Both of these objectives were woven together seamlessly in "Firefly," a humorous, ill-fated love story via Fallon McElligott.

In "Firefly," an arm is raised in the darkness, and a hand activates the IndiGlo watch face, which uses energy from the watch battery to light the dial. Suddenly, a firefly appears and begins to flirt with the watch as Frank Sinatra begins crooning "Strangers in the Night." At first, the hand gently swats the amorous firefly away. When the bug won't relent, the hand finally squashes it on the watch face, and the music grinds to a halt. Enter the voice of John Cameron Swayze: "Timex. It takes a licking and keeps on ticking." The spot, which broke in early 1992 on NBC's "Saturday Night Live," was named the best commercial of the year by Time magazine.

Although simple in concept, the commercial was technically very challenging— "a real head scratcher," says art director Dean Hanson, who teamed with copywriter Bruce Bildsten to create the spot, which was shot by director Bill George of Industrial Light and Magic. According to Hanson, the spot was filmed in layers with separate shots of the live-action hand, the illuminated watch band, and the animated hearts. In addition, the firefly was shot using motion-control cameras and a model; a computer-animated bug was not considered because it would appear to be "too cartoony," says Hanson.

The new product was introduced by the brand leader to diversify its line and offer consumers a wider variety of colorful, collectible watches like those popularized by Swatch. Timex, which applied the technology to 20-30 watch styles, was counting on the IndiGlo brand for its biggest revenue jump in 1993, according to Business Week.

Stores sold out of the watch following its introduction, sales doubled vis-à-vis the previous year, and the Middlebury, Connecticut company's offices received an unexpected number of phone calls. But perhaps the best testimonial to the technology can be recorded in human numbers. According to Business Week, when the World Trade Center was bombed in February 1993, a man led a group of people 34 floors in the dark to safety, leading them by the light of his IndiGlo watch.

Firefly
30 seconds
(SFX: Crickets chirping)
Title card: Timex introduces the IndiGlo night-light.
(SFX: Buzzzzzz & wings flapping)
Music: "Strangers in the Night"
(SFX: Splat!)
Music stops abruptly.
VO: Timex. It takes a licking and keeps on ticking.
Music: "Strangers in the Night" comes back up.

INDIGLO.
BY TIMEX

Client: Timex Corp.
Agency: Fallon McElligott,
Minneapolis, MN
Art director: Dean Hanson
Copywriter: Bruce Bildsten
Agency producer: Char Loving
Production company: Industrial Light
& Magic, Los Angeles
Director: Bill George
Animation: Tom Larson/Reelworks

Commercials for laxatives, douches, adult diapers and sanitary napkins typically use the same oblique formula for discussing personal body functions. They either inundate viewers with medical jargon, or show two friends confiding their intimate secret by the soft-focus seashore. Either way, humor is virtually absent from the picture, as is any semblance of acting talent.

That's why there were practically audible sighs of relief from the Casebook jurors when "Maureen and Her Daughter" was screened during judging. The commercial is the latest execution in a four-spot TV campaign for Sterling Health that uses sitcom-like scenarios and humor to sell Phillips' Milk of Magnesia laxative products. The campaign was headed by Ammirati & Puris creative directors Tod Seisser and Tom Nelson, who teamed

up for the first time to work on the campaign. They share creative credits with art director David Berger and copywriter David Wojdyla.

The star of the show is Maureen, a brassy, middle-aged "laxative evangelist," as Seisser describes her. Much to her family's chagrin, Maureen has no qualms about publicly discussing their bouts with constipation. The first spot in the campaign, "Raymond and Maureen," which broke October 1992, showed Maureen casually offering up Phillips' liquid to her husband and reminding him of his discomfort the previous evening. Embarrassed Raymond glances at the camera, saying, "We don't even know these people."

Seisser and Nelson came up with this approach because they themselves were uncomfortable discussing the subject. "Maureen is human,

she humanizes a problem that could be gruesome or scientific," explains Seisser. "The commercial acknowledges that not everyone spends their days talking about this problem." Subsequent commercials show Maureen dishing up similar advice to Raymond at a party and in a restaurant.

"Maureen and Her Daughter" followed in January 1993 to introduce MoM's new Gelcaps to a younger target audience. In the commercial, the mother-daughter duo are settling in their seats at a concert hall when Maureen brings up her favorite cause. She remains blissfully indifferent to her daughter's growing mortification. "We didn't have Gelcaps when I was your age," says Maureen. Her daughter wryly rejoins: "What did you talk about?"

Sterling Health banked on this serial approach to halt

Phillips' downslide in a marketplace where name brands are losing ground to generics and store brands. Before A&P won the account in 1991, the company had changed advertising campaigns frequently. The new campaign not only helped to reverse the slide, but helped Phillips to gain market share as well: Gelcaps in particular gained a full share point from competitive solid brands Ex-Lax and Correctol. In addition, the campaign began winning awards, such as a Bronze Lion at Cannes and a Gold Effie. Cast members were so popular, they received stacks of fan letters and even appeared on a talk show as their characters. Not a bad performance in an advertising category better known for making people squirm in their seats than sit up and take notice.

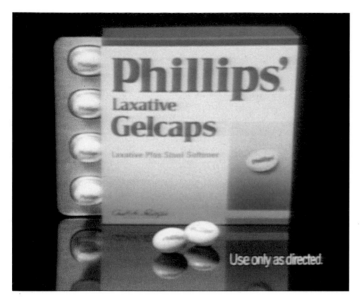

Maureen and Her Daughter
30 seconds
Maureen: Great seats. Comfy, hon?
Daughter: Yes, Mom.
Maureen: Good, 'cause you weren't last
night.
Daughter: When?
Maureen: When you were constipated.
Daughter: What?
Maureen: I think they had you in mind
when they came out with these new
Phillips' Gelcaps.
Daughter: Mother!
VO: Introducing Phillips' Gelcaps.
Laxative plus stool softener. Now,
trusted relief is yours in an easy-to-
swallow Phillips' Gelcap.
Maureen: We didn't have Gelcaps
when I was your age.
Daughter: What did you talk about?
VO: New Phillips' Laxative Gelcaps.
The modern answer to an age-old
problem.

Client: Sterling Health
Agency: Ammirati & Puris, Inc., New
York, NY
Art director: David Berger
Copywriter: David Wojdyla
Creative directors: Tom Nelson, Tod
Seisser
Agency producer: Jack McWalters
Production company: Rick Levine
Productions, New York, NY
Director: John Massey

"New York, New York" is the quintessential anthem of the American dream. When its lyrics are sung by New York City homeless people, however, the song becomes a painful reminder that for thousands, the "city that doesn't sleep" is inhabited by people who shiver all night on park benches.

This heartstring-tugging irony drives "New York, New York," a 60-second public service announcement for the Coalition for the Homeless. The spot was created by Streetsmart Advertising, an ad hoc agency comprised of Leslie Sweet, a freelance art director, and Peter Cohen, an art director and senior vice president/group creative director at Lowe & Partners SMS. The commercial shows one homeless person after another singing portions of the song: a woman sitting in her wheelchair in the rain; an older man wiping his eyes in grief. The commercial fades to black and ends with this silent message in titles: "It's up to you, New York, New York" above the Coalition's phone number.

Casting street people to sing the song in the commercial helped put a human face on homelessness, says Sweet, but also made it devastating to shoot. "It was one of the most emotionally draining experiences of my life," she says. "At night, I would go back to my apartment and look around at what I had and realize that you just can't take all this for granted."

The direction was key to the spot's effectiveness, she

Streetsmart sniped the cardboard boxes in storefronts to make a chilling point.

says. If people sang the song joyfully, the commercial would appear to be a parody. With director Laura Belsey, the team explained their intentions to the 35 people they filmed for the spot. Each of them understood the irony, notes Sweet, who brushes aside the criticism in the media that they had been exploited. "If we are out there to help them, why would we want to manipulate them?" she asks.

"New York, New York" was inspired by "Cardboard Box," an earlier Streetsmart spot that shows a steady shot of a homeless person curled up in a cardboard refrigerator box while a super muses, "Something's wrong when Frigidaire and Westinghouse do a better job of housing the homeless than New York City." That commercial in turn was inspired by an intrusive print campaign Sweet and Cohen had previously devised, in which a batch of corrugated boxes bearing the same message were sniped on walls around the city. All three efforts—the two television spots and the cardboard boxes—were selected for this Casebook.

When considering music

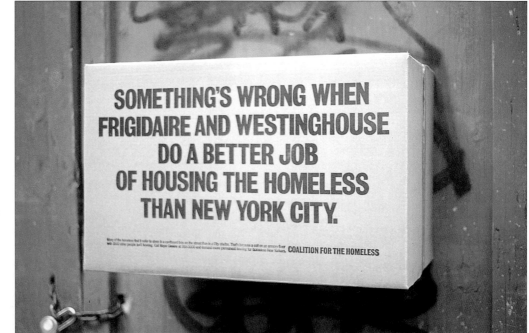

SOMETHING'S WRONG WHEN FRIGIDAIRE AND WESTINGHOUSE DO A BETTER JOB OF HOUSING THE HOMELESS THAN NEW YORK CITY.

COALITION FOR THE HOMELESS

Cardboard Box
30 seconds
(SFX: City sounds: cars, wind, footsteps and a garbage truck grinding its load.)

for "Cardboard Box," the team investigated using the song "New York, New York" as an ironic counterpoint. When they landed recording rights to the song, however, Cohen and Sweet decided it seemed to diminish, instead of enhance, an already strong message. So they decided to maximize the song's potential and created a new commercial. "Cardboard Box" was backed with the sound effect of a garbage truck grinding its contents.

In addition to helping increase donations to the Coalition, "New York, New York" won top honors at every major advertising award show in 1993, including a Gold Pencil and Best of Show at the One Show, three Gold Awards at the Art Directors Club Awards, a Silver Pencil at D&AD in London, and the prestigious Gold Lion at the 40th Annual International Advertising Film Festival at Cannes. In addition, the cardboard box and the "New York, New York" spot are now part of the the Museum of Modern Art's permanent advertising and graphic design collection.

But Streetsmart found their biggest reward far from the limelight. While filming homeless people cooking dinner over a barrel under the Brooklyn Bridge, Belsey was offered a plate of food. "Here are these people with nothing, and they are offering you all they have," says Sweet. "It was amazing to me."

New York, New York
60 seconds
(SFX: Music comes up)
Homeless man 1: Start spreadin' the news. I'm leavin' today. I want to be a part of it.
Homeless man 2: New York, New York.
Homeless man 3: I want to wake up in a city that doesn't sleep…
Homeless man 4: …and find I'm king of the hill…
Homeless man 5: …top of the heap.
Homeless man 6: These little town blues are melting away.

Homeless woman: I'll make a brand new start of it in old New York.
Homeless man 7: If I can make it there, I'll make it anywhere…
Title card: It's up to you New York, New York.

Client: Coalition for the Homeless
Agency: Streetsmart Advertising, New York, NY
Art directors/copywriters: Leslie Sweet, Peter Cohen
Directors: Leslie Sweet, Peter Cohen ("Cardboard Box"), Laura Belsey ("New York, New York")

Boy Is That an Ugly Shirt

"Boy, is that an ugly shirt," a musician told Glenn Hale, glancing at the thrift-store Hawaiian schmatte he was wearing one night at Up & Under, a Milwaukee blues bar. Inspiration struck. Hale, a freelance advertising copywriter/producer, thought the playful insult would make a brilliant retailing gimmick. He formed Wise Guise, Inc. to manufacture a whole line of tacky shirts, or "visual assaults," as he calls them. "These are shirts you can spot 50 yards away," he says.

Before the shirts were even manufactured, Hale hooked up with his former agency Hoffman, York & Compton and persuaded them to take him on as a client. These posters, mailed to local buyers in early 1993, were created as a teaser campaign in the truest sense, as the shirts were not shipped until almost a year later. Curiously, the ads were also placed in the November issue of Balloon Life magazine.

According to HY&C creative director Tom Jordan, the campaign had to convey a certain irreverence to appeal to the target audience of young adults and teenagers. "You have to be cool to wear these," agrees Hale. Posters emphasize the shirts' garish colors by superimposing images of them on breathtakingly beautiful stock shots of nature: A sunset saturated in reds and oranges has an Ugly Shirt tacked on the image with the headline, "Some colors take your breath away. We're looking for people to lose their lunch."

Store buyers' initial reaction was incredulous, says Hale, but many others showed interest. Hale wishes to create limited editions of the shirt to turn them into collectibles. He thinks his approach is effective, because the marketing angle is so strong. As evidence, he points out the number of companies who make "millions and millions of widgets" but go under because they can't market themselves properly. He feels his backwards approach is preferable. "A shirt's a shirt," says Hale. "What differentiates us is the name and the attitude we're selling it with." Talk about truth in advertising.

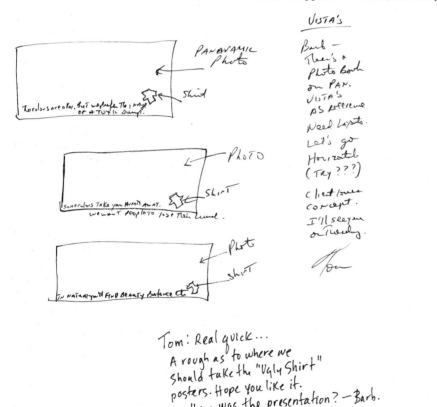

Early sketches for Wise Guise reveal a dialogue between the copywriter and art director.

Some colors take your breath away. We're looking for people to lose their lunch.   BOY IS THAT AN UGLY SHIRT.™

In nature you can find beauty, balance, and subtle color. Frankly, we don't get it.   BOY IS THAT AN UGLY SHIRT.™

The colors are okay. But we'd prefer the image of a toxic dump.   BOY IS THAT AN UGLY SHIRT.™

Client: Wise Guise, Inc.
Agency: Hoffman, York & Compton, Milwaukee, WI
Art director: Barb Paulini
Copywriter: Tom Jordan
Creative director: Tom Jordan
Photographers: Koji Yamashita, Mitsuo Kazama/Panoramic Images

"This stuff is straight out of James Bond movies," says copywriter Carolyn Strickland, describing the surveillance and monitoring devices for sale at Spy Factory, a national chain with a franchise in Atlanta. Wares include a "nanny-cam" for spying on babysitters, "bionic" hearing aids, stun guns, and bulletproof clothing.

Given the serious, high-tech nature of the equipment, Spy Factory wanted an advertising campaign that would make those products seem less intimidating and more accessible. Strickland and her Cole Henderson Drake partners—copywriter Kim Genkinger and art director Peggy Redfern—met that

criteria by creating a campaign using dark humor in clever headlines. Two of those ads, which broke in Creative Loafing, Atlanta's alternative newspaper starting in Summer, 1992, were chosen for this Casebook.

For one ad, the team borrowed a theme prevalent in classic detective stories—infidelity. The headline reads: "Where To Shop For Your Husband And His Girlfriend," followed by, "With our huge selection of surveillance and monitoring devices, we've got a sneaking suspicion you'll find just what you're looking for."

A second ad brashly invites kleptomaniacs to pay a visit. The headline reads:

"Shoplifters Welcome. After All, We've Got To Try This Stuff Out On Someone." Body copy reads: "...if necessary we'd be happy to demonstrate."

Unfortunately, someone took Spy Factory up on that offer. Using a book purchased at the store about breaking and entering, a thief broke into the store one night and robbed it. The perpetrator was caught, but store owners were clearly embarrassed. "That's not really something they like to talk about," says Strickland. Nevertheless, store traffic did increase after the ads ran—with paying customers, of course.

Client: Spy Factory
Agency: Cole Henderson Drake, Atlanta, GA
Art director: Peggy Redfern
Copywriters: Carolyn Strickland, Kim Genkinger
Creative director: Dick Henderson

Shoplifters Welcome. After All, We've Got To Try This Stuff Out On Someone.

We carry only the most sophisticated surveillance, monitoring and protectional devices. And, if necessary, we'll be happy to demonstrate.

Spy Factory

3872 Roswell Rd., Atlanta, GA 30342
(404) 814-1136

Where To Shop For Your Husband And His Girlfriend.

With our huge selection of surveillance and monitoring devices, we've got a sneaking suspicion you'll find just what you're looking for.

Spy Factory

3872 Roswell Rd., Atlanta, GA 30342
(404) 814-1136

Most dog food commercials either hype the "meaty goodness" in their brand by showing glossy-coated golden retrievers chowing the stuff down in great gulps; or placing dogs in cute or goofy situations while a voiceover drills the brand name ("kibbles and bits, kibbles and bits") mercilessly ("kibbles and bits, kibbles and bits") into your skull.

By contrast, this television campaign introducing Ralston Purina's Nature's Course dog food focuses on what is not found in the bowl, such as preservatives, food coloring and pesticides. This information is conveyed using the familiar dry humor and restraint for which the agency, Fallon McElligott, is known. Simplicity counted, since each of the three spots—"Fly," "Rigid," and "Living Color"—are only 15 seconds long.

Each commercial humorously spoofs the distasteful effects those additives wreak on living things. In "The Fly," a housefly lands on a bowl of dog food, takes off, then drops dead from the pesticides. "Rigid" shows a dog so pickled with preservatives his owner can lift him up by the tail when she vacuums. And artificial colors in "Living Color" turn a Dalmatian's spots into a rainbow of hues. This tack was taken to prove to premium dog food consumers that this dry dog food is superior because it uses only natural ingredients, according to art director Dean Hanson, who worked with copywriter Phil Hanft on the campaign. "Basically, two things are important to people about dog food: taste and diet," says Hanson. "This campaign bridged both concerns." The new product was created to compete with Iams and Science Diet, two natural dog foods sold through veterinarians' offices. After the campaign broke, Nature's Course achieved a two per cent market share in grocery stores.

Director Mark Coppos was selected to shoot the campaign because of his sense of timing and the ability to keep his cool with animals—"He doesn't go ballistic on the set," as Hanson notes. In "Rigid," casting took on a whole new meaning. Looking for a stiff dog, the creative team first contacted local taxidermists, but quickly found that profession steers clear of stuffing house pets. "It also wouldn't be real politically correct," says Hanson, so a prop was quickly substituted.

The Fly
15 seconds
(SFX: Buzzing)
VO: Too many pesticides in your dog's food?
VO: There are no pesticides in new Nature's Course.

Living Color
15 seconds
VO: Too many artificial colors in your dog's food?
VO: There are no artificial colors in new Nature's Course.

Rigid
15 seconds
(SFX: Vacuum)
VO: Concerned about artificial preservatives in your dog's food?
VO: There are no artificial preservatives in new Nature's Course.

Client: Ralston Purina Co.
Agency: Fallon McElligott, Minneapolis, MN
Art director: Dean Hanson
Copywriter: Phil Hanft
Creative director: Pat Burnham
Production company: Coppos Films
Director: Mark Coppos

Tiny Mythic Theatre Company

"The universe of people who go to these plays is very small," says Nick Cohen, describing the audience for the obscure, avant-garde theater groups his agency, Mad Dogs & Englishmen, has counted as clients. Cohen is not kidding. While attending a Pointed Stick Theatre Company production that his actress-wife appeared in several years ago, he counted just 10 other people rattling around the empty theater. The problem, he says, was not bad acting—just bad marketing. "These theater people are good at putting on their own performances, but they are not good at promoting them," he observes.

Cohen feels that one way to expand that universe is by creating theater advertising that breaks all the rules. That means posters with no pretentious plot summaries or wanky, surreal photography. In the early 1990s, MD&E created a series of witty, offbeat posters for Pointed Stick Theatre Company that spoofed the genre by appealing to people on a baser level. Many of them employed a single, attention-grabbing headline. The plot of Shakespeare's *A Midsummer Night's Dream*, for example, was summarized as, "Fairy Queen in Donkey Sex Scandal."

The posters drew audiences to the theater, awards to the agency, and the interest of the Tiny Mythic Theatre Company, which was suffering from a similar identity crisis. Cohen agreed to take them on as a client, but only if they permitted the

Our latest production deals with...well...you know.

ETHEL MERMAN

Frankenstein. The Musical. Feb 22-Mar 10. Ohio Theatre.

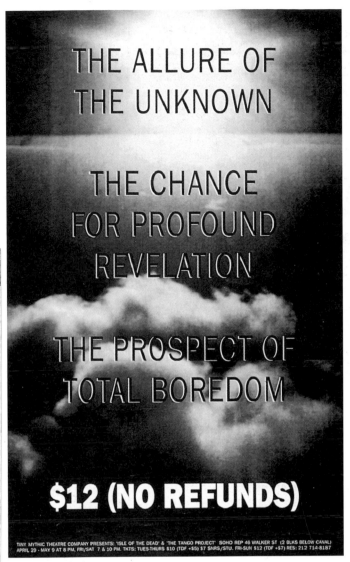

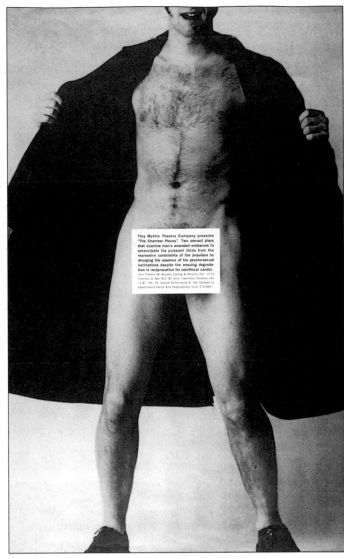

agency to have complete editorial control over the ads' content. Cohen has a pragmatic attitude about appealing to New York City's cynical downtown denizens: "Basically, people think theater is boring. All they want is the promise of a good night out."

The Casebook judges obviously felt this formula was effective. No fewer than eight Tiny Mythic Theatre Company posters were selected to appear in this Casebook. Each one enjoyed a two-month run on walls downtown, before they were covered up by other snipers.

The posters employ the New York Post school of sensational headline-writing by focusing on certain lewd and sensational aspects of a play. A photo of two copulating turtles illustrates the production of *Obscene* and *Las Sirenas*, with the headline: "Our Latest Production Deals with...Well...You Know." For *The Chamber Pieces*, a flasher's private parts are obscured by a block of type with this erudite description of the play: "Two one-act plays that examine man's amended endeavors to emancipate his puissant libido from the repressive constraints of the populace by divulging the essence of his psycho-sexual inclinations despite the ensuing degradation in reciprocation for zenithical candor."

Other ads in the series blatantly warn of the prospect of boredom from attending an avant-garde production. A poster for *Isle of the Dead* and *The Tango Project* features a sun beaming from behind clouds with a headline promising: "The Allure of the Unknown. The Chance for Profound Revelation. The Prospect of Total Boredom. $12 (No Refunds.)" Similarly, the poster for *A*, a "carnival adulteration of Nathaniel Hawthorne's *A Scarlet Letter*, promises: "5 minutes of profound insight into the wretched, judgemental [*sic*], hate-filled nature of man," followed by, "1 hour, 37 minutes of twenty-four people running around doing silly things in their underwear."

Apparently, this irreverent approach worked. After the campaign broke, attendance at the theater grew to 85 per cent. The troupe is doing well enough to have opened a 10,000-square-foot performance complex in partnership with another theater company in SoHo.

Cohen regards billboard advertising as an effective, exciting medium that offers a world of creative opportunities. "It's like street art," he says. "It's like a community bulletin board. There are no rules: Everything is fair game." That must explain why a poster for *The American Living Room* spoofs the medium itself by posing as a citation from the Sanitation Department. The canary-yellow ad blares: "This Poster Is A Violation of NYC Dept. of Sanitation Code #1-8075." It asks that all complaints be referred to "Tiny Mythic Theatre Company," except, of course, during the days when the theater is performing the show.

5 minutes of profound insight into the wretched, judgemental, hate-filled nature of man.

TINY MYTHIC THEATRE COMPANY PRESENTS "A", A CARNIVAL ADULTERATION OF NATHANIEL HAWTHORNE'S "THE SCARLET LETTER" OHIO THEATRE
66 WOOSTER ST SOHO NYC MAY 7 - 24 8PM (EXCEPT MON) TUES - THURS $10 (SNRS & STUDENTS W/ID $7 TDF ACCEPTED) FRI - SUN $12 RES: 212 274 9807

1 hour, 37 minutes of twenty four people running around doing silly things in their underwear.

TWO HOURS OF AIR CONDITIONING* ONLY $7

TINY MYTHIC THEATRE COMPANY PRESENTS **THE AMERICAN LIVING ROOM - A DIRECTING CABARET** - 27 PIECES BY 27 DIRECTORS - JULY & AUGUST
SATURDAY & SUNDAYS - OHIO THEATRE - 66 WOOSTER ST NYC - FIRST COME/FIRST SERVED - DOORS OPEN 8PM - TICKETS $7 (TDF +$2) - INFORMATION 212 274 9807

PASSION CONFLICT VIOLENCE DEATH

Tiny Mythic Theatre Company present BLOOD WEDDING
by Federico Garcia Lorca   Ohio Theatre   66 Wooster St
SoHo   New York City   Mar 8th-18th   Tues-Sun 8 pm
Senior Citizens $6   Students $6 (weeknights/with ID)
Mar 14 "Fiesta" Benefit $25   Res: (212) 645 5143

$10 (including light refreshments).

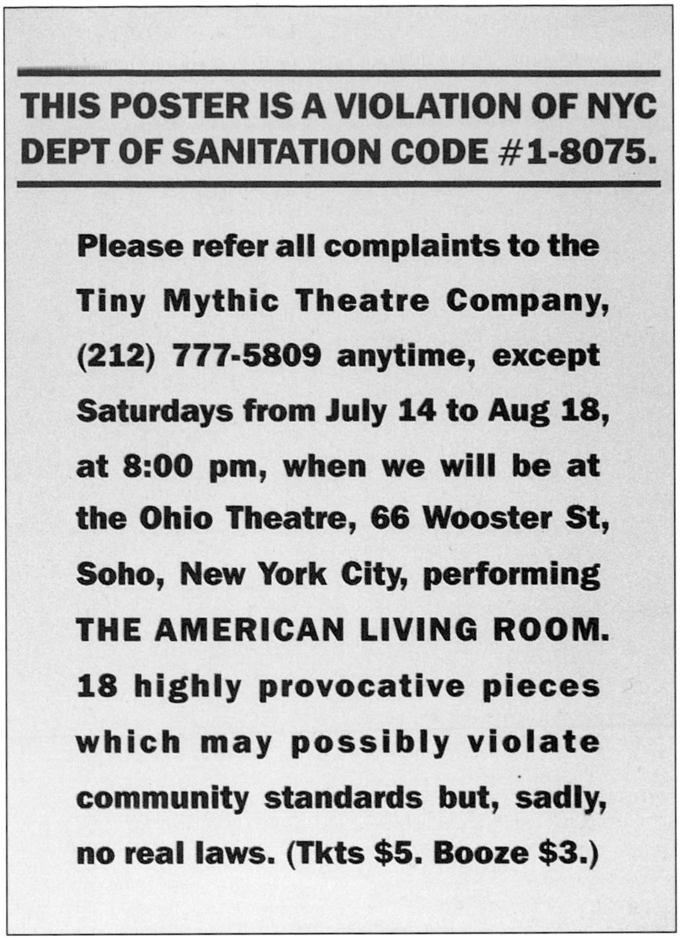

THIS POSTER IS A VIOLATION OF NYC DEPT OF SANITATION CODE #1-8075.

Please refer all complaints to the Tiny Mythic Theatre Company, (212) 777-5809 anytime, except Saturdays from July 14 to Aug 18, at 8:00 pm, when we will be at the Ohio Theatre, 66 Wooster St, Soho, New York City, performing THE AMERICAN LIVING ROOM. 18 highly provocative pieces which may possibly violate community standards but, sadly, no real laws. (Tkts $5. Booze $3.)

Client: Tiny Mythic Theatre Co.
Agency: Mad Dogs & Englishmen, New York, NY
Art directors: Taras Wayner ("The Chamber Pieces"); Nick Cohen (all others)
Copywriters: Ty Montague ("The American Living Room" [Sanitation Code]; "Frankenstein"; "Obscene" and "Las Sirenas"); Mikal Reich ("A"; "The American Living Room" [Air Conditioning]); Shalom Auslander ("Isle of the Dead" and "The Tango Project"); Courtney Rohan, Amy Heller ("The Chamber Pieces")
Creative director: Nick Cohen
Photographer: Ian Rubin ("Frankenstein")

Is bigger better? This campaign for The United Way of Metropolitan Atlanta aims to prove so. As part of the country's largest, most comprehensive charitable organization, the Metropolitan Atlanta chapter supports 77 area health and human service agencies. To encourage donations from local residents, the chapter wanted to instill trust in potential donors and assure them that their donation would go a long way and truly reach someone in need.

Given the breadth of this directive, the creative team at Fitzgerald & Company worried that it would be difficult to find an emotional hook to compel people to give, says art director Kim Cable. "Our mission was to communicate the scope of the organization, but we felt that made it so far removed from people," she says. "We decided to break it down into categories to personify the problems that exist." These included the elderly homeless (shown here, in the ad selected by the Casebook judges), family welfare, AIDS and health and rehabilitation. The campaign consisted of five print ads and four television spots and broke in 1991 in newspapers, TV, outdoor and transit.

Cable acknowledges the difficulty in finding a balance between sentiment and sensationalism when attempting to raise public awareness of human suffering. Using overt humor or shock tactics seemed too extreme to be effective. Initially, Cable and copywriter

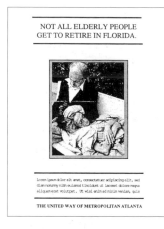

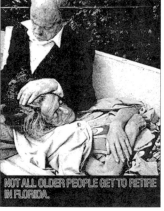
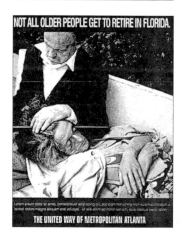
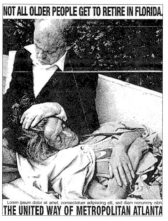
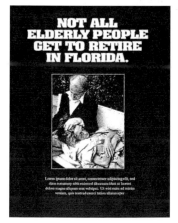

Early comps (above) show experimentation with the scale of the photograph and the type. The final ad maximizes the impact of a poignant image.

Guy Lowe realized that the account would offer them a good shot at winning awards, but they knew in good conscience that they had to resist emulating award-winning formulas simply for the sake of gaining professional recognition: "It didn't make sense to be outrageous for the sake of being outrageous," she says.

Their campaign forces viewers to confront their own ignorance and prejudices in ads that balance dark humor in headlines with startling images. For example, a poster for AIDS reads: "Homo Sapiens. The only group that can get AIDS." For children's welfare, an ad is headed, "More fathers run away from home than children do."

To illustrate the ad depicting the elderly homeless population, Cable wished to find a candid photograph of real people. Although the pro bono budget didn't allow for original photography to be commissioned, she found the shot she wanted in the book *Homeless in America*. The photographer, James Conroy, agreed to accept a stock fee for its use in the ads.

After the campaign broke, donations went up in the Atlanta area, exceeding the 6 per cent growth the chapter had ambitiously projected. This increase was the highest among all national chapters of United Way.

Reflecting on the campaign, Cable challenges the notion that pro bono clients offer agencies creative carte blanche: "Pro bono is difficult to do," she says. "The approval process is easier, but there is so much good pro bono work out there, you really have to put your imagination to work to break through."

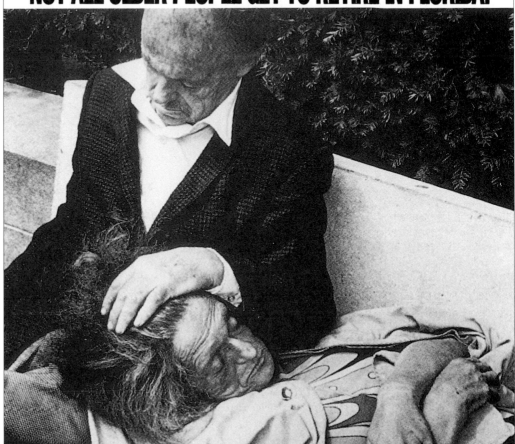

NOT ALL OLDER PEOPLE GET TO RETIRE IN FLORIDA.

The Elderly. Children At Risk. Families In Crisis. The Hungry And Homeless. AIDS Crisis Fund. Health And Rehabilitation. There's One Way To Help In Lots Of Ways.

THE UNITED WAY OF METROPOLITAN ATLANTA.

Client: The United Way of Metropolitan Atlanta
Agency: Fitzgerald & Co., Atlanta, GA
Art director: Kim Cable
Copywriter: Guy Lowe
Creative director: Jim Paddock
Photographer: James Conroy

People don't need to see the movies *Single White Female* or *Sea of Love* to get the willies about placing personals ads. That uneasiness has always existed, especially when it comes to finding a love interest through the paper.

This newspaper campaign for the Minneapolis Star Tribune's "Get Acquainted" personals section uses wry humor to try to alleviate those fears. Created by Fallon McElligott, the campaign ran for six weeks in the Star Tribune's pages. It matches up bold, witty headlines with personals ads concocted by Fallon creatives. One ad headlined "Need a Lawyer?" reads, "ATTORNEY, 37 and single, tired of all court and no courting." Body copy tells us that the Tribune's new voice mail system makes it easy to "meet exactly the type of people you'd like to." Another ad notes dryly, "When a guy answers your personals ad, at least you know he can read."

"Our job was to convince people that it's okay to place a personals ad," says art director Bob Brihn, who teamed with copywriter Mike Lescarbeau. (Brihn has since left Fallon for Cole & Weber, Seattle.) "We wanted to bring some relief to the trauma by showing problems common to dating in general."

The sample ads are aimed at a straight, white-bread, middle-of-the-road audience—and are definitely rated PG, unlike those in the Village Voice, where a full page dedicated to "Anything Goes" reads like the guest list on a daytime talk show. But as Brihn points out, the Tribune

ROSES ARE RED, VIOLETS ARE BLUE, YOU CAN RUN A PERSONALS AD, EVEN IF YOU CAN'T WRITE GOOD.

You don't need a way with words to run an ad in Get Acquainted. All you need is to want to meet people. Or whatever. Call 673-9015 for details, today.

"Get Acquainted" in the **Star Tribune**

"HEY, CHECK OUT THE ADJECTIVES ON HER."

With our new voice mail system, the Star Tribune makes it easy to meet the kind of people you like. Call 673-9015 for sincere, honest, outgoing, friendly details today.

"Get Acquainted" in the **Star Tribune**

MEN AREN'T REALLY A DIME A DOZEN. BUT IT'S CLOSE.

For the price of the Star Tribune, you can meet all kinds of men. And you can get an even cheaper date by running an ad of your own. Call 673-9015 for details today.

"Get Acquainted" in the **Star Tribune**

is a midwestern family newspaper. "Is it raw as personals go? No," he says. "But what you see there is on the edge for these guys."

NEED A LAWYER?

With our new voice mail system, the Star Tribune is making it easy to meet exactly the kind of people you'd like to. Call 673-9015 for details today.

"Get Acquainted" in the **Star Tribune**

WHEN A GUY ANSWERS YOUR PERSONALS AD, AT LEAST YOU KNOW HE CAN READ.

Looking for a well read person? With a readership of over one million, the Star Tribune helps you reach the people who share your interests. Call 673-9015 for details today.

"Get Acquainted" in the **Star Tribune**

Client: Star Tribune
Agency: Fallon McElligott, Minneapolis, MN
Art director: Bob Brihn
Creative director: Pat Burnham
Copywriter: Mike Lescarbeau
Photographer: Joe Lampi
Typographer: Bob Blewett

Rarely does an account executive—or a client, for that matter—get credit for inspiring the idea behind an ad campaign. But Hoffman, York & Compton creative director Tom Jordan believes in giving credit where credit is due. He says the idea of morphing two personalities for this For Color, Inc. print ad was the brainchild of a "suit"—account executive Todd Treleven.

Long before the ad was created, Treleven got his kicks around the office by splicing together photos of different people in the agency and pasting them on the walls with suitable labels. Thus, a creative director/account exec combination was "the ultimate presenter"; and two art directors together became "the ultimate art director." "It would look really comical," says Jordan. When For Color, a local color separator, wanted an ad demonstrating the retouching capabilities of its new Sigmagraph System 6000 Mark II, a high-end electronic imaging system, Treleven's collages came immediately to mind as the perfect solution. The direct mail poster was aimed at art directors and production professionals at local graphic design and publishing firms.

Famous and infamous couples were considered as candidates for digitization. The field was narrowed due to estate costs, or, in one case, sensitive circumstances: While the agency was working on blending Ferdinand and Imelda Marcos, the former Philippines president was reported to be dying, so the agency decided to drop the idea. Charles and Diana were substituted (but long before the royal marriage broke up). Together with For Color, art director Mike Wheaton worked to blend skin tones and backgrounds. The resulting "Charles and Di" elicited a number of phone calls from curious clients, as well as an inquiry from a German magazine that wanted to run the image on its cover. Jordan nixed the idea. "We didn't think it would really help the color separator or us," he says.

Although the agency has considered following up with a composite of the President and First Lady and calling it "Billary," at this point, they feel the joke's stale, since many magazines have co-opted the technique since their first ad was mailed. "We got to the point where we said, 'This has been done. Let's do something else,'" Jordan says.

Before the royal breakup, HY&C merged Charles and Di for one last tête-à-tête. Along the way, they also melded Imelda and Ferdinand.

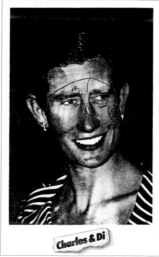

AS BROUGHT TOGETHER by the Sigmograph System 6000 Mark II at ⊕ FOR COLOR INC. Color separations for offset & gravure; 400 S. 5th St., Milwaukee, WI 53204 414-273-4992 Toll Free 1-800-877-7023.

Client: For Color, Inc.
Agency: Hoffman, York & Compton, Milwaukee, WI
Art directors: Mike Wheaton, Todd Treleven
Copywriter: Mike Wheaton
Creative director: Tom Jordan

Edgar Allen Poe is reputed to have been a drug-addicted, half-crazed alcoholic who died penniless and drunk in a Baltimore gutter. Although Poe is not around to personally enjoy it, this print campaign from The Martin Agency cleans up that unsavory image to attract visitors to the Poe Museum in Richmond, Virginia, the city where the writer lived during the early 19th century. Before the campaign appeared in local college newspapers, the scholarly museum had an identity problem of its own. "There was a real low awareness of the museum in Richmond," says art director Cliff Sorah. "We really had to start from scratch."

The ads portray Poe as an innovative literary pioneer who deserves to be remembered in a positive light. Lengthy copy by Raymond McKinney humorously corrects common misconceptions about his character and emphasizes his literary contributions. One ad headlined "Sadomasochist, drug addict, manic depressive, pervert, egomaniac, alcoholic? When did Poe find time to write?" argues that while Poe did behave erratically, many rumors about him were largely untrue, having been spread by Rufus Griswold, his unscrupulous literary executor. Another ad notes that Poe is credited with inventing an entire literary genre—the detective story— in 1841, with the publication of the short story "The Murders in the Rue Morgue."

Besides achieving a measure of notoriety during his short lifetime, Poe was also panned by many critics in the American press: One Boston newspaper called *The Raven and Other Poems* "a parcel of trash." Abroad, however, his fame attained "Michael Jackson proportions," according to a third ad headlined "Early Americans called Poe a hack. The French loved him. (Does this mean we'll be opening a Jerry Lewis museum one day?)"

The agency resisted peppering the ads with excerpts from Poe's works, since the museum has a broader scope. "The museum also has a lot of displays about what Richmond was like in the early 19th century," says Sorah. "We wanted to show that the museum has historical as well as literary appeal."

Poe created the detective story back in 1841. (Just think how many butlers would be roaming the streets today if he hadn't.)

It was a dark and stormy night in April 1841. The latest issue of Graham's magazine had just hit the streets. And there, nestled between a verse entitled "An April's Day" and music to "Oh! Gentle Love", appeared a quirky little story called "The Murders in the Rue Morgue".

The publication called it a "tale of ratiocination" (the word "detective" had not been coined yet). Poe understatedly called it "something in a new key."

Something in a new key, indeed. In a few short pages, he created one of the most popular literary (and later film) genres of all time.

The story introduced a scholarly recluse by the name of C. Auguste Dupin who had a "peculiar analytic ability." And he put it to good use by solving a particularly brutal murder that had the local police baffled. (The culprit, incidentally, turned out to be a trained orangutan).

Poe went on to pen three more tales of ratiocination. Not only were they highly entertaining, they also introduced many future clichés to the detective business.

For example, the old crime being committed in a locked room scenario. The frame-up. Postmortem examination and ballistic evidence. The "least likely murderer" ploy. Poe even outfitted Dupin with a pipe.

(The murderous orangutan of "The Murders in the Rue Morgue", while a groundbreaking first, has yet to resurface in any later works.)

Obviously, if you've ever cracked an Agatha Christie novel, flipped on a Columbo movie, or ever played a game of Clue, these plot devices are quite familiar.

In fact, Sir Arthur Conan Doyle, creator of Sherlock Holmes and perhaps Poe's most famous disciple, said that "if every man who owed his inspiration to Poe were to contribute a tithe of his profits therefrom, he would have a monument greater than the Pyramids..."

Alas, not everyone has done so, so we'll have to do with our quaint little Poe Museum. Why don't you come check it out? You can wander through the Old Stone House, Richmond's oldest surviving dwelling, study "The Raven" illustrations and see plenty of other mysterious things.

We could give you the address, but why don't you figure it out for yourself. (Here's a clue- it's right here in Richmond, near Church Hill) **The Poe Museum**

The Edgar Allan Poe Museum, 1914 East Main Street, Richmond, Virginia 23223. Open 7 Days A Week. Admission $5.00. Call (804)648-5523.

Early Americans called Poe a hack. The French loved him. (Does this mean we'll be opening a Jerry Lewis museum one day?)

After reading Poe's poem "Al Aaraaf", a Baltimore critic wrote "all of our brain-cudgelling could not *compel* us to understand it."

A review in Boston's *The Morning Post* of his *Tales of the Grotesque and Arabesque* cried, "A greater amount of trash within the same compass it would be difficult to find."

The Boston Post called *The Raven and Other Poems* "a parcel of current trash."

And perhaps the most acidic attack came from the *New York Tribune* on the day of Poe's funeral. "Edgar Allan Poe is dead...This announcement will startle many, but few will be grieved by it." Tough crowd.

Meanwhile, over in France, Poe's reputation was hitting Michael Jackson proportions. One reviewer wrote "this Poe is a fellow of great acuteness and spirituality."

In fact, the whole country adored him. He inspired a whole generation of artists.

So why did we scoff at him back here at home?

Perhaps because Poe didn't have a whole lot in common with other American writers of his day.

Just contrast the rugged American feel of James Fenimore Cooper's *The Last of the Mohicans* with any of Poe's tales of madness, decay and death.

Or consider Longfellow, Emerson and Thoreau. They wrote of great, wide-open spaces. Poe wrote of tombs.

Poe was different, and different can be hard to accept.

Now throw in an unscrupulous literary executor who took advantage of his position to slander Poe's life and work. What you end up with is a genius who got a pretty raw deal while he was living.

Today, of course, Poe is a national figure. His fiction has drawn a larger international audience than that of any other American writer. Poe is probably chuckling in his grave (that's a metaphor he would have liked).

Why don't you stop by The Poe Museum at 1914 East Main Street? You can enjoy our slide show about Poe's life and take a tour through a model of what Richmond was like in Poe's day. And we promise, no Jerry Lewis exhibitions yet. **The Poe Museum**

The Edgar Allan Poe Museum, 1914 East Main Street, Richmond, Virginia 23223. Open 7 Days A Week. Admission $5.00. Call (804)648-5523.

Client: The Poe Museum
Agency: The Martin Agency, Richmond, VA
Art director: Cliff Sorah
Copywriter: Raymond McKinney
Print producer: Kay Franz

These ads for Teva Sport Sandals vibrate with the visual equivalent of audio feedback: they're loud, raw and visceral. They're in your face. "Now that is fresh work," remarked one Casebook judge when reviewing this print campaign from Stein Robaire Helm.

Aimed at young, male, "extreme" outdoor enthusiasts, the ads were infused with attitude because that audience automatically tunes out ads with an overt sales pitch, says art director Kirk Souder. Since competitors Nike and Timberland were far outspending them, Teva (pronounced "TEH-vah") needed a campaign that would make up in spirit what it lacked in dollars. The upstart shoe company was started by Mark Thatcher, a Colorado River guide/geophysicist, who designed the strappy sandals after the cut-up sneakers he and friends wore years ago when proper shoes for white-water rafting were nonexistent. Today, this style of sandal is joining Birkenstocks as a popular warm-weather alternative to sneakers.

At first, the client resisted using edgy, distorted photography that would largely obscure the product, especially since this was their first campaign. Eventually, however, they sensed that the approach was on target. "They realized what they were selling was attitude and lifestyle," says Souder. Photographer Mark Hanauer shot these water-drenched shots of Teva-wearing athletes in Hawaii and used a cross-

LIFE FROM INSIDE A SHOE. *Life from inside a Teva.*

YOU PROBABLY HAVE A PAIR OF SENSIBLE SHOES. *But what do you wear when you've lost all your senses?*

processing developing technique to saturate the color and further rev up the energy. "We wanted something frenetic and kinetic," says Souder, who teamed with copywriter Court Crandall on the campaign. (The two have since left Stein Robaire Helm to form their own agency, called Ground Zero.)

Copy is irreverent and advocates a carefree existence with the theme, "Do you exist in shoes or live in Tevas?" One ad, for example, is headed, "When you die, they'll put you in a shiny suit. As if death didn't suck enough already." (One consumer was particularly taken by the ad, since he was both a Teva wearer and a funeral director.) The campaign's tone echoes two other recent consumer goods campaigns aimed at the same audience: Reebok's "Life's Short. Play Hard"; and Pepsi's "Be Young. Have Fun. Drink Pepsi."

Ads ran in Rolling Stone, Outside and Sports Illustrated in 1993. Following the campaign's launch, the company retained its lead in the sport sandal category despite aggressive marketing by its heavy-hitting competitors.

Client: Teva
Agency: Stein Robaire Helm, Los Angeles, CA
Art director: Kirk Souder
Copywriter: Court Crandall
Creative directors: Kirk Souder, Court Crandall
Photographer: Mark Hanauer

Cowboy songs, elegant typefaces, funky animation: These are not ingredients normally found in recipes for health-related public-service announcements, especially for a subject as serious as giving blood. But that's exactly why they were used in this television campaign for Memorial Blood Center of Minneapolis from McElligott, Wright, Morrison, White, an agency that has since closed shop. These unexpected, sophisticated elements work equally to entertain and draw attention to the urgent need to donate blood at a time when supplies have hit a record low nationwide. The approach is a refreshing change from most health-related PSAs, which use the grim reaper approach to motivate people to action.

Taking an artistic, not an antagonistic, approach gives the audience more credit for intelligence, says Jean Rhode, who worked as copywriter on all three spots. "We didn't want anything that said, 'You're the next to die.' We wanted to be smarter than that and not play with people's emotions."

Each commercial is visually—and emotionally—distinct. In "Gurney," art-directed by Leslie Sweet and directed by Tony Kaye, a twangy cowboy song about waiting interminably plays while the camera sweeps down a long, empty hospital corridor and finally rests on a small child, who looks plaintively up from her gurney. Titles read: "If you think it's scary giving blood, try waiting for it."

Humor and irony are used

to motivate potential donors in "Anything but Love," an all-type :30 which empathizes with people who are weary of giving handouts. For this, British type designer Jonathan Barnbrook created black-and-white titles with words set in elegant typefaces that emerge and fade seamlessly from one frame to the next, each time mentioning a different charity needing cash: "The March of Dimes needs your money," "The Arthritis Foundation needs your money," etc. Suddenly the music screeches to a halt and the last sentence crashes to the bottom of the screen, leaving behind a period that transforms into a throbbing red heartbeat. A closing title reads: "We Don't. Give Blood."

A third spot, "Photocopy Jazz," art-directed by John Morrison, features the animation of Chel White, a Portland, Oregon director who manipulates photocopied images. Colorized shots of mouths, torsos, fists and faces flash by in a surreal, elliptical tapestry to a hip-hop/jazz score. "Medical technology can copy almost anything," reads the closing titles. "Except Blood."

Although the creative team is unsure about the impact the campaign had on increasing donations, they do know the Blood Center was pleased with the work, since it ran the spots for a year and asked for additional outdoor print work to supplement the television portion.

While the commercials incorporate an unexpected mix of visuals and music, serendipity was involved in

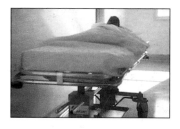

shooting them as well. Because of a big Minneapolis snowstorm, the creative team was able to borrow Kaye, the award-winning British director, who was stranded in town after shooting Village Inn restaurant commercials for the agency. After looking over the boards for "Gurney" and "Anything," he offered to direct them, and volunteered his friend and collaborator, Jonathan Barnbrook, for the type treatments in "Anything." Although Leslie Sweet was thrilled with their contributions, she emphasizes that the best PSAs rely on a big idea, not necessarily a big-name director. "Sometimes when you have the least money, you do the best work," she says.

Gurney
30 seconds
(SFX: Twangy, bluegrass music)
VO: Weary blues from waitin'. Lord, I been waitin' too long. These blues have got me cryin'.

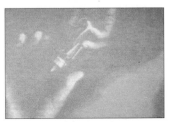

Anything But Love
30 seconds
(SFX: Music comes up on the song "I Can't Give You Anything But Love")
VO: I can't give you anything but love. Baby, baby. That's the only thing I've plenty of, baby. Dream awhile, scheme awhile, you're sure to find…
(SFX: Heartbeat)

Photocopy Jazz
30 seconds
(SFX: Sound of a copy machine making a copy which leads into jazz music.)

Client: Memorial Blood Center of Minneapolis
Agency: McElligott, Wright, Morrison, White, Minneapolis, MN
Art directors: Leslie Sweet ("Gurney," "Anything But Love"); John Morrison ("Photocopy Jazz")
Copywriter: Jean Rhode
Production companies: Tony Kaye Films, Chel White Films
Directors: Tony Kaye ("Gurney," "Anything But Love"); Chel White ("Photocopy Jazz")

"When a guy hauls out a $40 bottle of bourbon for his friends, he wants to tell the story behind it," says Fallon McElligott copywriter Mike Lescarbeau. "There's a b.s. factor involved."

Sit down a spell, because that story, as told in this newspaper ad campaign from Fallon McElligott, is long-winded and colorfully embellished. It's about Booker's Bourbon, a premium, small-batch straight bourbon from Jim Beam brands, named after Booker Noe, great-grandson of Jim Beam and the master distiller at the company's digs in Clermont, Kentucky.

Like Frank Perdue, Dave Thomas, and Tom Carvel, Booker Noe has a down-home, folksy manner that personifies the product. Watching the portly Southerner on Jim Beam sales tapes in their Minneapolis offices "got our blood rushing," says Lescarbeau. "He's got some personality. When he drinks the bourbon, he swirls it around in this brandy snifter and really enjoys the hell out of it."

Body copy in the print ads attempts to replicate those sensory pleasures by leading readers on a one-on-one tour with Booker Noe through the company's grounds and barrel-lined warehouses. We learn that Booker's is pricier because it is distilled longer than most bourbons—six to eight years, compared to the regulation two to four. It is uncut and unfiltered and ranges from 121 to 127 proof. Then, of course, it is personally tasted by Booker Noe, who makes sure that it has reached its peak perfection. He takes this responsibility seriously, as we read in one ad: "Booker Noe pauses along a gravel road in

the grounds of the Jim Beam Distillery in Clermont, Kentucky, rests his bigger-than-life hand on a cane, and gazes up at a warehouse that holds hundreds of barrels of aging bourbon. 'Nothing could possibly make a man feel richer,' he says, 'than knowing he's got the best whiskey there is.'" The campaign, created to appeal to upscale single malt-whiskey drinkers, ran in 1992 in The Wall Street Journal.

One would think Lescarbeau spent many hours by Noe's side to capture the essence of the man, but, in fact, he never left Minnesota. The night before he and art director Susan Griak were to leave for Kentucky with photographer Craig Perman, Lescarbeau was in a car accident. So Griak and Perman set up shots and brought back photographs and videotapes for Lescarbeau to work from.

Long copy and a complicated layout, together with an extremely hands-on Jim Beam marketing department, made the approval process difficult. "Mike was rewriting forever," says Griak, who adds that the client "hates showing maps" in ads and until the last minute refused to allow Noe to be photographed at his favorite fishing spot (the creative team ultimately prevailed). Noe, of course, took

it all in stride, in his slow, easy manner. One can picture clearly Noe's response when asked to pose at the pond with his pole: "'Course I will."

Client: Jim Beam Brands Co.
Agency: Fallon McElligott, Minneapolis, MN
Art director: Susan Griak
Copywriter: Mike Lescarbeau
Creative director: Pat Burnham
Photographers: Kerry Peterson (bottle shot), Craig Perman (all other photographs)

Windsor Canadian

"Brown goods"—marketing-speak for liquors such as whiskey and bourbon—are outsold by "white" liquors like vodka and gin by about 40 million cases a year. Although Adweek recently reported a tiny gain in sales for the category in 1992, brown goods marketers have an uphill battle as tastes continually drift toward the clean and clear.

Some brands choose to speak directly to the core audience of older whiskey drinkers with traditional, hearth-and-home imagery; others try to wean the so-called "X" generation from their spritzers and coolers to more hardy fare with sexy or humorous image campaigns.

Jim Beam's Windsor Canadian whiskey is a middle-of-the-road "brown" with a hard-working, middle-of-the-road audience. Although it is the 15th-selling whiskey in the country, it is the best-seller in Minnesota, North and South Dakota and Nebraska. In this print campaign created by Fallon McElligott for national newsweeklies, Windsor aimed to broaden its appeal to that market without necessarily bringing the kids along for the ride. Research showed that the whiskey was not a special-occasion drink, but bought to stock the liquor cabinet. For this reason, client and agency decided to focus on what motivates one to relax with a drink, instead of showing how it can enhance one's social standing—the kind of image art director Tom Lichtenheld describes as a "happy white-people ad."

Together with the client, the creative team wanted to illustrate how the product is a reward for "putting up with life's everyday irritants," says Lichtenheld, who with copywriter John Stingley, parlayed this directive into the headline, "Fortunately, every day comes with an evening."

The idea was sparked by a news photo Lichtenheld had filed away years earlier in which a man was shown struggling to shove a massive line of grocery carts back into the supermarket. This photojournalistic approach was admired by one Casebook judge, who remarked enviously, "Everyone in advertising dreams of using it."

With art buyer Michaelanne Gillies, the team searched through stacks of back issues of News Photographer magazine for still shots to pursue for the theme. In addition, they solicited 50-60 newspapers for submissions. They came up with a series of 11 print ads with scenes from everyday life: a man stuck between subway doors, firemen doing incessant drills, a woman languishing at the returns desk at a department store. Lichtenheld admits that several of the shots, although inspired by real news photos, were staged. One original photo showing a child walking on the fresh cement his father was laying, for example, was reshot, substituting a dog because the client and agency felt that the image of a child was inappropriate for liquor advertising.

After the campaign broke, the client received hundreds of requests for reprints, and sales were reported to be up by double-digits.

Fortunately, every day comes with an evening.

Fortunately, every day comes with an evening.

Fortunately, every day comes with an evening.

Fortunately, every day comes with an evening.

Fortunately, every day comes with an evening.

Fortunately, every day comes with an evening.

Fortunately, every day comes with an evening.

Fortunately, every day comes with an evening.

Fortunately, every day comes with an evening.

Fortunately, every day comes with an evening.

Client: Jim Beam Brands
Agency: Fallon McElligott, Minneapolis, MN
Art director: Tom Lichtenheld

Copywriter: John Stingley
Photographer: Dave Jordano (product shot)

The Village Voice in Manhattan has always knocked the Establishment with its radical coverage of social issues, politics, media and culture. That's why Mad Dogs & Englishmen got a little rambunctious themselves when creating a subscription ad campaign to increase the weekly's circulation base. True to the spirit of the agency's name, the ads read like the polished prose of Oscar Wilde while delivering the bite of a belligerent bulldog.

"@*!# off, you establishment-bracing pseudo-anarchists and take your money-hungry subscription offer with you," rants one ad, "…you've all gone softer than the over-fed bellies of the crooked middle-aged babykissing handshakers you so hypocritically condemn." A check box beneath this diatribe offers another option: "Yes, I want to buy a year subscription to the Village Voice." Like others in the campaign, this ad humorously exposes the underlying pretensions of the Voice from the cynical, skeptical point of view of its readers, especially suburbanites in the tri-state area who read the Voice to stay connected. Their disdain for the Voice's snobbery is revealed in another ad that reads, "Hell, I wouldn't have my home contaminated with a subscription to your elitist rag if you were giving away five-speed blenders." Another ad sneers at a holiday subscription offer that cuts a "measly" 22 per cent off the regular subscription price. "Yeah, I got your 'special offer'

right here, pal," it says.

Alas, readers are not spared, either. Right-wing yuppies who hide their secret passion for the paper are skewered in another effort: "My skin crawls just thinking about the kind of looks I'd get if my neighbors knew that I indulged in your 'alternative' publication…first the BMW goes down the pooper in the 'crash' and now you want to rob me of what little standing I have left in society." On the other extreme are the New Age tree-huggers who are slammed in an ad that agonizes about the helpless trees felled for the sake of the paper. "You strip off the skin and grind its flesh into a sappy pulp," sobs the copy. "Then you dance on its grave by printing your petty witticisms on the remains." The ads were written by Mikal Reich and Shalom Auslander, who teamed with art directors Nick Cohen and Taras Wayner.

Mad Dogs principal Nick Cohen knew their impertinent approach would sell to management because "the newspaper is honest," he says. "It really stands behind the freedom of the writers, even when they criticize the management itself." The agency landed the account when Cohen convinced management that they could create a campaign that would effectively increase subscriptions and replace a blow-in rely card that cost the paper $150,000 a year. One year after the campaign broke, the Voice saw a 30 per cent increase in subscriptions, which surpassed all its expectations.

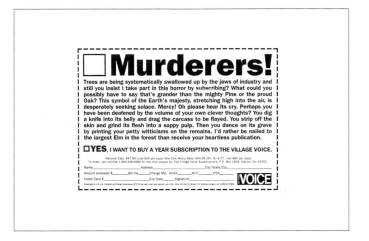

Naturally, Voice staffers did resist some of the more unflattering ads in the campaign. "At times, the editorial staff thought the ads were very derogatory toward the writers," says Cohen. "But we felt the whole idea of the Voice is to challenge the status quo. Therefore, nothing is sacred."

Situations Wanted Ads

To increase advertising revenue in its classified pages in 1991, the Village Voice revamped its "Situations Wanted" section to appeal to New York's droves of unemployed workers. The newspaper offered readers a free four-week ad in the section. They would be given a phone mailbox where interested employers could reply to the ads and the advertisers could retrieve their messages at a cost of 79 cents per minute.

To raise awareness of the special offer, art director/ principal Nick Cohen and copywriters Mikal Reich and Shalom Auslander created a series of funny, phony classified ads to run in the section. Some of them mocked New York's ubiquitous out-of-work artists looking for day jobs to support their craft. For example, a Shakespearean actor seeking a waiting job pleaded his case thus: "Hark! I beseech thee, fore not a beggar nor vagrant I,…I beg of you; grant respite within your good premises." A "dog walker/poet" likewise expresses his talents in another ad: "He strainfully let go. It fell gently to the folded paper. A moist smack." Other efforts reveal a DMV worker

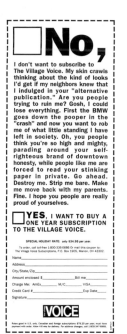

SITUATIONS WANTED

Hark! I beseech thee, fore not a beggar nor vagrant I, But art now, and not by choosing, without haven of a guild. I beg of you; grant respite within your good premises.
ACTOR SEEKS RESTAURANT POSITION. ☎ 5802

Place a **FREE** Situations Wanted ad for 4 weeks in our Help Wanted Classified Section. Someone out there is desperate to hire someone with your qualifications. To place an ad call 212-475-5555. **VOICE**

SITUATIONS WANTED

SOCIAL WORKER. If I don't get a job soon I'll kill myself. ☎ 2876

Place a **FREE** Situations Wanted ad for 4 weeks in our Help Wanted Classified Section. Someone out there is desperate to hire someone with your qualifications. To place an ad call 212-475-5555. **VOICE**

SITUATIONS WANTED

He strainfully let go. It fell gently to the folded paper. A moist smack.
DOG WALKER/POET ☎ 3423

Place a **FREE** Situations Wanted ad for 4 weeks in our Help Wanted Classified Section. Someone out there is desperate to hire someone with your qualifications. To place an ad call 212-475-5555. **VOICE**

SITUATIONS WANTED

Ex-DMV clerical worker seeks position. But I'm in no hurry. ☎ 9876

Place a **FREE** Situations Wanted ad for 4 weeks in our Help Wanted Classified Section. Someone out there is desperate to hire someone with your qualifications. To place an ad call 212-475-5555. **VOICE**

"in no hurry" to find a job; and a social worker threatening to commit suicide.

According to Cohen, the campaign was "a complete success and a total failure." The advertisements successfuly increased the "Situations Wanted" section from two column inches to two full pages of advertising. But it was a "total failure" because the Voice soon discovered that it was making more money from people checking for messages than from employers leaving messages. "People were getting annoyed," says Cohen, so the Voice, fearing a negative backlash, dropped the section.

Client: The Village Voice
Agency: Mad Dogs & Englishmen, New York, NY
Art directors: Nick Cohen, Taras Wayner
Copywriters: Mikal Reich, Shalom Auslander
Creative director: Nick Cohen

"The Washington Post owns the market in the D.C. area," says art director John Morrison about the Capital's venerable daily newspaper. "But research showed that younger people felt it was a 'gray old lady' with no relevance to them. We wanted to create a campaign which would tell them, 'If you don't read this paper daily, you're out of the loop.'"

DDB Needham's 1991 television campaign for the Post consisted of man-on-the-street testimonials about reasons for reading the paper, focusing less on its acclaimed international coverage than on its softer, more accessible offerings, such as sports, the horoscope and lifestyle features. This campaign helped "put a face" on the paper, says Morrison, so a follow-up campaign in 1993 could be "more assumptive" and leave more creative options open for the agency to communicate the same message.

"Virgo" was part of that effort. Created to increase home delivery sales to area adults aged 25-39, the spot combines tension and humor to pique curiosity about the Post's coverage. The commercial opens on a sunny, tree-lined suburban street. As the camera slowly pans from house to house, a woman's voice delivers an emotionless capsule review of that day's news. "Today it will be warmer than yesterday," she intones, "A trusted man in the public eye has lied for personal gain." The locked-down shot of the street is intercut with flashing images

of a person preparing to leave for work: A hand is turning a door knob; pulling out keys. As a car pulls out of a driveway, the voiceover says, "If you are a Virgo it is a good day..." Suddenly the car crashes into another in the street. "...to stay home," she says. Titles read: "The Washington Post. If you don't get it, you don't get it." The commercial was written by freelance copywriter Scott Burns and directed by Mark Coppos of Coppos Films, Los Angeles.

The commercial's use of tension-building, fleeting images, combined with an understated, almost inaudible voiceover, help make it a bit cryptic, and therefore longer-lasting, says Morrison. "We wanted to give people a reason to watch," he explains. "It's not until the third or fourth time people see it that it really sinks in."

Apparently, the spot sank in effectively. Qualitative research showed record awareness for the paper after the campaign was launched. In addition, the creative team claims that the campaign's theme, "If you don't get it, you don't get it," has become "practically a household phrase."

Virgo
60 seconds
(SFX: Birds chirping)
VO: A local man has lost his dream....A popular brand of toothpaste is on sale....A small part of your brain is in charge of making you age....Today it will be warmer than yesterday....A trusted man in the public eye has lied for personal gain....Last night's victory ended a three game skid....If you're a Virgo...
(SFX: Car headlight smashing.)
VO: ...it's a good day to stay home.
Super: If you don't get it, you don't get it.

Client: The Washington Post
Agency: DDB Needham, New York, NY
Art director: John Morrison
Copywriter: Scott Burns
Production company: Coppos Films
Director: Mark Coppos
Production company producer: Michael Appel
Post-production house: Lost Planet
Editor: Hank Corwin

Lee Jeans

"This campaign is an advertising guy's dream," says former Fallon McElligott art director Michael Fazende. "Whenever you have a villain to pick on all day long, it makes your job easy."

In this five-spot campaign for Lee Jeans' Easy Riders, the villain is bad-fitting jeans, an enemy lurking in almost anyone's closet. The commercials, which parody people struggling into their jeans, are part of Lee's long-running campaign that uses humor to position the blue jeans as "the brand that fits." The Easy Rider brand is Lee's "relaxed fit" line created for the over-30 set, who can no longer fit into the Levi's they wore in college. The commercials broke during the 1992 Olympics.

Focus groups gave Fazende and copywriter Mike Lescarbeau an idea of how emotionally connected people are with their jeans. Women in particular revealed the creative lengths they will go to get their jeans to fit, such as using pliers to pull up zippers or pressing wet cloths on thigh areas to stretch them out. With these scenerios in mind, the team had plenty of material to play with. In "Button," a man's button pops off his jeans and ricochets wildly like a bullet around the living room. In the absurdly funny "Roommate," a woman keeps her date waiting downstairs so long during her quest to find properly-fitting jeans that when she finally emerges, he is exchanging vows with her roommate in a living room crowded with wedding guests.

The team wanted the spots to be funny, but not always at the expense of someone's weight problem. "Women are burdened with such body image problems in this country, so we wanted to be sensitive of that," says Lescarbeau. "There's a line you can't cross," he notes, adding that whenever they did, it was usually at the expense of "some poor guy," such as in "Inhale," where a man sucks in his gut so hard a room's entire furnishings are pulled toward him.

Since the commercials are mostly dialogue-free, the creatives chose British commercials director Roger Woodburn of Park Village Productions to shoot them because of his sense of humor, casting ability, sense of timing and down-to-earth style, which Lescarbeau describes as "anti-style style." Casting proved to be a challenge. The creative team wanted "real" people, not thin models, but the client insisted that the performers be svelte in order to make the product look good.

Even so, the team feels the spots achieved a sense of realism that balances the zany humor. "They're not beautiful-looking commercials; they're not beautifully lit, because basically we didn't want them to have a particular style," says Fazende. "The whole idea was to tell a story and not let anything get in the way, to play off the gags in it."

Button
30 seconds
(SFX: Background noise, TV audio)
(SFX: "Bang" of button flying off)
(SFX: Cowboy movie ricochets, etc.)
VO: Need a little more room in your jeans? Try Relaxed Fit Jeans, from Lee.
Super: The brand that fits.

 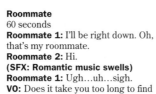 

Roommate
60 seconds
Roommate 1: I'll be right down. Oh, that's my roommate.
Roommate 2: Hi.
(SFX: Romantic music swells)
Roommate 1: Ugh…uh…sigh.
VO: Does it take you too long to find jeans that fit?
(SFX: Footsteps coming down stairs. Music for the wedding march comes up.)
VO: Get the jeans that fit the first time. Relaxed Fit Jeans from Lee.
Super: The brand that fits.

Shower
30 seconds
(SFX: Male tenor sings Italian aria)
(SFX: ZZZZZZIP!)
(SFX: Male voice replaced by soprano)
VO: Need a little more room in your jeans? Try Relaxed Fit Jeans from Lee.
Super: The brand that fits.

Silhouette
30 seconds
Music: Loud rock music.
Woman: Ohh!
MVO: Trouble getting into your jeans?
MVO: Try Relaxed Fit Jeans, from Lee.
Super: The brand that fits.

Inhale
30 seconds
(SFX: Inhaling and exhaling sound)
**(SFX: Bird chirping in
background)**
MVO: Trouble getting into your jeans?
(SFX: Bird chirping)
MVO: Try Relaxed Fit Jeans from Lee.
Super: The brand that fits.

Client: The Lee Company
Agency: Fallon McElligott,
Minneapolis, MN
Art director: Michael Fazende
Copywriter: Mike Lescarbeau
Agency producer: Judy Brink
Production company: Park Village
Productions, London
Director: Roger Woodburn

Farm at Mt. Walden

The same year Robert Redford's *A River Runs Through It* romanticized the sport of fly fishing on celluloid, The Martin Agency in Richmond, Virginia hooked into its allure in print for the Farm at Mt. Walden, a gourmet food company specializing in smoked trout.

These ads for Mt. Walden feature gently-lit photographs of antique rods and fancy lures to convey the purest essence of catching fish. These images by local photographer Tony Sylvestro reflect the old-fashioned sensibilities of the client, who eschews artificial ingredients and commercial processes to cure their products. "We wanted the ads to be classy but also very homey and unmechanized," says Richard Plà-Silva, a principal of Mt. Walden, who founded the company with Kyle Strohmann. Subtle humor in copy reinforces this message. One ad with a colorful array of fishing lures, for example, is headlined: "Deception, trickery, artificial ingredients. Things you build a business on." The point-of-purchase posters were mailed to food distributors and specialty shops beginning in Spring 1992.

Initially, the client was reluctant to omit product shots and play down the brand name in the ads, especially since the company was new and had not done any previous advertising. In the late 1980s, Plà-Silva and Strohmann had bought the eponymous farm in Rappahannock County, Virginia's lush horse country, and had begun producing small batches of smoked trout

WHAT HUCK FINN WOULD'VE DONE, IF HE'D GONE TO HARVARD BUSINESS SCHOOL.

WHEN WE STARTED THE BUSINESS, YOU COULD ALMOST HEAR THE TROUT LAUGHING.

WHY NOT START A BUSINESS? WE ALREADY HAD THE OFFICE EQUIPMENT.

DECEPTION. TRICKERY. ARTIFICIAL INGREDIENTS. THINGS YOU BUILD A BUSINESS ON.

to sell at a local farmers' market. Long lines began to form at the stand, and after a feature story about the trout ran in the Washington Post in 1990, the business took off. Now, the company distributes a full line of smoked products nationally through specialty food stores and upscale catalogs like Williams-Sonoma, and has moved the operation to a renovated gas station in The Plains, Virginia. It was there that Martin's then creative director, Bill Westbrook, discovered the company and asked to take them on as a client.

This is an image campaign designed for retailers' walls, so the product name is almost unnoticeable. In these two posters, the name Applewood Smoked Virginia Trout appears only in tiny script below an engraving of a trout within the company's logo. The mark itself is very discreetly tucked at the bottom right corner of the page. But Plà-Silva knows first-hand the value of soft-selling upscale brands. Before starting the company, he was creative director at Plà/Mauro, an agency which handled advertising for restaurants and caterers. He recognized that images of fishing would be more appealing than showing the fish themselves. "There's only so much you can show of smoked trout," says Plà-Silva delicately.

Client: Farm at Mt. Walden
Agency: The Martin Agency, Richmond, VA
Art director: Mark Fuller
Copywriter: John Mahoney
Creative director: Bill Westbrook
Agency print producer: Jenny Schoenherr
Photographer: Tony Sylvestro

The Sunset Marquis Hotel and Villas

"The IBM guy coming to Los Angeles on business is not going to stay at the Sunset Marquis," says art director Michael Fazende, describing the glitzy Hollywood hotel favored by rock musicians, actors and other leather-motorcycle-jacket types. The hotel checks in so many rock groups, in fact, that it recently built a recording studio right in the basement, complete with a video connection to a lobby bar where patrons can savor the action with their Absolut.

Realizing the cachet of a colorful clientele, Fazende and his Fallon McElligott partner Mike Lescarbeau played up this attraction to their peers in a black-and-white trade campaign appearing in Adweek, The Hollywood Reporter and Variety in 1993. Many of the ads are type-driven, with a single, tongue-in-cheek headline, such as "More tattoos per guest than any other hotel," and, "Do we protect the privacy of our guests? What guests?" Headline type was set in Snell Roundhand, an ironically elegant typeface for such a grungy message. This was a deliberate attempt to show both sides of the hotel, says Lescarbeau. "There's a rough edge to the clientele, but the hotel is very elegant," says Lescarbeau, "so Mike's type choice was perfect."

Previously, the hotel ads and brochures stressed its elegance and exclusivity, an approach which did little to set it apart from other local hosteleries. "We thought they had more personality than

that," says Fazende, who has since left Fallon to work at Scali McCabe Sloves in New York.

That personality was given a (stubbled) face by Dallas photographer Richard Reens, who is best known for shooting tattooed Harley Davidson riders. Texas nightclubs were scoured for candidates: In one shot, five Guns 'N' Roses types sneer seductively from behind rivers of cascading hair in an ad promoting the hotel's "Free Shampoo." Another ad likens a zombie-like Gothic rock fan to "Your Procter & Gamble client, after a week at the Sunset Marquis." The creatives had no problem coming up with the character composite; while staying at the hotel in the past, they had rubbed elbows with the likes of Bruce Springsteen, Jeff Beck, Phil Collins and the late River Phoenix.

Although submitted by Fallon, the campaign is technically a freelance assignment that the team landed while staying in town for a commercial shoot. Because the hotel is frequently used by the agency, the duo was on friendly terms with the owners and sales staff. They landed the account in true Hollywood style: While power-breakfasting at poolside, the Sunset Marquis' director of sales sidled up to them and mentioned that the hotel could use a new logo or letterhead. "Of course, we said, 'Gosh, why don't you do some ads?' recalls Fazende.

Free Shampoo.

Sunset Marquis Hotel And Villas.
Unique. Even By Hollywood Standards.

In California
people do in
hotel rooms what
they'd never do
in public.

Work.

Too shy to use a laptop by the pool? We'll provide any business equipment you need in the privacy of your suite or villa. That way nobody has to know you work for a living.

Sunset Marquis Hotel And Villas.
Unique. Even By Hollywood Standards.

Do we protect
the privacy
of our guests?

What guests?

At the Sunset Marquis, we've helped some of the world's most prominent celebrities get away from it all. For example, last week, well....nevermind.

Sunset Marquis Hotel And Villas.
Unique. Even By Hollywood Standards.

Client: Sunset Marquis Hotel and Villas
Agency: Fallon McElligott, Minneapolis, MN
Art director: Michael Fazende
Copywriter: Mike Lescarbeau
Photographer: Richard Reens, Dallas, TX

Wrangler

Wrangler clothing is as much a part of a rodeo cowboy's ensemble as his hat, boots and stamina. For 46 years, the company has been an official sponsor of the Professional Rodeo Cowboy Association. The clothing truly is authentic: Pockets and rivets on blue jeans, for example, are specially designed for rough rides. That kind of authenticity appeals to dudes as well: Wrangler is the number one brand of Western wear in the country.

Previously, Wrangler communicated their leadership position in advertisements featuring world champion rodeo stars as endorsers and models. When Wrangler asked The Martin Agency for a new draft of the campaign in 1992, art director Cliff Sorah and copywriter Steve Bassett decided to buck that trend for a fresher approach. "So many people use endorsers that way," says Sorah. "We didn't want to do that."

Instead, Sorah and Bassett changed the perspective, by showing us what they imagine to be the rider's point of view. In this print ad and poster campaign running in Pro Rodeo Sports News, off-camera rodeo stars are merely implied, from their terrifying point of view on the bull. From that vantage point, everyone seems to be wearing Wrangler clothing and a scared look on their faces. Headlines identify the product and the endorser, such as: "A Colorful Selection of Brushpopper Shirts, As Viewed by Clint Corey, World Champion Bareback Rider."

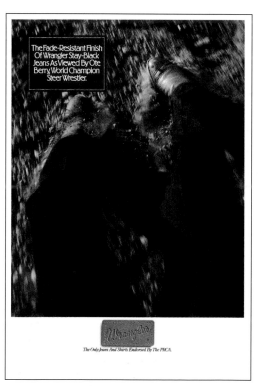

The campaign was photographed by Brian Lanker using real rodeo fans in Walla Walla, Washington.

The idea is taken one step further in an ad that features a blurry shot of a cowboy's backside as he scurries away from a charging animal. The headline: "Wrangler Authentic Cowboy Cut Jeans As Viewed by Outlaw Willie, Rodeo Bull."

Fortunately, Wrangler hasn't taken the same kind of beating as rodeo cowboys get in the arena. Sales have increased steadily in the past few years, up 20 per cent in 1991 and 30 per cent in 1992, the year this campaign ran.

Checotah Shirts

Like the Wrangler jeans and shirts campaign, the poster for Wrangler's fade-resistant Checotah shirts uses an unexpected visual to communicate a message instantly.

This time, the device

Fade Resistant Checotah Shirts.

The Western Original

Fade-resistant Checotah shirts and jeans.

ghost the remaining image on a Quantel Paintbox at 10 per cent increments at a time. Ironically, the campaign initially was to include mention of the Stay-Black jeans as well, but shadows blended on the jeans and horses, making it impossible to mask the pants out realistically. The creative team was also limited to using images photographed during a shoot set up for a public relations campaign. The image was shot near Santa Fe, New Mexico by photographer Mark Scott.

Looking back on his work, Meagher is satisfied with the effectiveness of the image, but he still has ideas about taking the joke one step further: "Now, I think we should have faded down the headline and logo," he says, hastening to add, "as long as you'd still be able to see it."

works to humorously promote the colorfast benefit of Wrangler's vivid Checotah line of shirts: Four cowboys are shown riding their horses on the range. Everything in the poster is as faded as John Wayne's jeans except, of course, the shirts themselves. According to Martin Agency art director Bob Meagher, the client wanted to focus on this attribute, since a previous campaign had emphasized the shirts' bright colors and styling. The posters were created as a point-of-purchase piece for Western wear stores.

While "washed out" images in print pieces are normally the bane of an art director's existence, this time Meagher spent hours finessing the color to reach an ever-lighter shade of pale. He had a professional color separator mask the shirts and

Jeans and Shirts
Client: Wrangler
Agency: The Martin Agency, Richmond, VA
Art director: Cliff Sorah
Copywriter: Steve Bassett
Agency print producer: Jenny Schoenherr
Photographer: Brian Lanker

Checotah Shirts
Client: Wrangler
Agency: The Martin Agency, Richmond, VA
Art director: Bob Meagher
Copywriter: Steve Dolbinski
Agency print producer: Jenny Schoenherr
Photographer: Mark Scott

When Mercedes-Benz began searching for a new agency to handle its $100 million-plus account in early 1992, it was with the realization that sales had tumbled from 78,375 in 1990 to 58,868 at the end of 1991. The drop was due to the recession and increased competition from newly-introduced, lower-priced luxury cars such as Nissan's Infiniti and Toyota's Lexus. For many years, McCaffrey & McCall had emphasized Mercedes' superior quality with the campaign theme, "The best-engineered car in the world." In the 1990s, the German car manufacturer clearly needed more to convince buyers to spend $50,000 and up for a luxury car during rough economic times.

Each of the agencies invited to compete in the pitch agreed that the car had to be made more accessible. As one Mercedes marketing executive told Forbes in an interview shortly after the account review, "All the agencies who competed for the account told us to loosen up and get a life."

The agency that argued this point most convincingly was Scali McCabe Sloves. The New York shop was awarded the $90 million national account, and its Richmond, Virginia subsidiary, The Martin Agency, was handed the $40-million dealer account. The joint effort would simultaneously stress Mercedes' key selling points—safety, longevity and resale value—while giving it a warmer image.

This newspaper ad from Martin for the 300D exemplifies this approach.

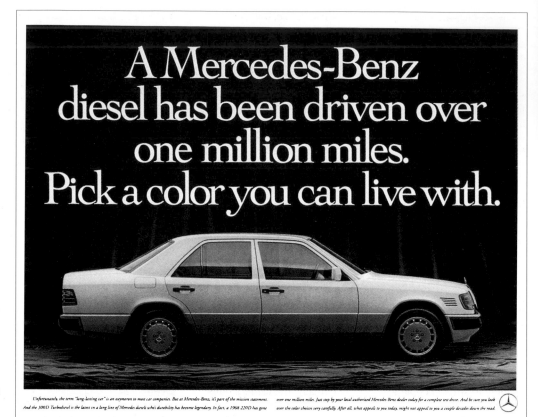

Created to sell a diesel car targeted to 35- to 54-year-old adults with household incomes of $100,000 and more, the ad stresses the car's key feature—longevity—with a touch of humor. Research had shown that some Mercedes diesel cars, with their long-lasting, efficient diesel engines have been driven more than one million miles. This ad delivers that information with the advice: "Pick a color you can live with." The ad broke in newspapers in State College, Pennsylvania. "If there's ever an indestructible car, it's the Mercedes," says art director Mark Fuller, who teamed with copywriter Joe Alexander. "We wanted to remind people that somewhere out there is a car that has been driven longer and faster than any other car."

Fuller and Alexander have since created "hundreds" of ads for the client. Fuller says each offers its own particular challenge. "All the good automotive work has been done," he says. "How many different ways can you talk about speed and performance?"

Client: Mercedes-Benz
Agency: The Martin Agency, Richmond, VA
Art director: Mark Fuller
Copywriter: Joe Alexander
Creative director: Kerry Feuerman
Agency print producer: Karen Smith
Photographer: Michael Furman

"New Yorkers are a jaded bunch. They know their chances of winning the lottery are about as good as getting hit by lightning," says copywriter Paul Spencer. Since New York State has one of the oldest lottery systems in the country and more than its share of big-city cynics, sales of the twice-weekly Lotto jackpot tickets were in a slump in the recessionary early 1990s. New York State Lottery needed a fresh way to revive sales.

In previous years, DDB Needham tempted New Yorkers to play Lotto with a campaign themed "All You Need is a Dollar and a Dream" and commercials featuring man-on-the-street interviews with people fantasizing about striking it rich. Although the campaign was popular, it eventually became stale after years of use. A new effort needed to focus more on winning to attract people who play on an impulse, explains Spencer. "'Dollar and a Dream' got across the point that playing was fun," he says. "But we said, 'Let's have fun with what you might do after you won.'"

Spencer and DDB Needham art director David Angelo decided to spin fantasies of wealth while not over-promising the odds of winning. The line, "Hey, You Never Know," seemed to have just the right shrugging tone. The team also came up with a variation on the previous theme, with the line "What a difference a dollar makes," but they nixed it because, as Spencer explains, "It seemed like it was crafted by the copywriter."

From there, the team created a print and advertising campaign in which ordinary people remain humble and unaffected by their new lush surroundings, often to comical effect: In print ads, an elderly Chinese man in traditional costume beams while sitting on top of his speedboat; a "generation X"-er barbecues in front of his manor home; a golden retriever rides in a limousine pulling a tacky pink camper. In :15 commercials, a nerdy man commands his driver to drive ever-faster in circles, and a couple stand with a real estate agent in front of an enormous mansion, inquiring whether it comes equipped with cable television.

Longer commercials take a more story-telling approach: "Opera," shot by Brent Thomas of Coppos Films, features an older woman knitting to the strains of opera. Eventually, the camera pulls back to show that she's not listening to the stereo, but rather a live orchestra in her living room. In "Grand Ball," the arrival of royalty is heralded by a prim butler, who then announces the next guest: "Bob of Buffalo." Similarly, in "Bradford Manor," a commercial shot by John Lloyd of Limelight Productions, a tour group passes through the vast halls of a stately manor house that appears to be a museum until they reach the living room, where they find the Bradford family curled up by the television.

Spencer's favorite is the Lloyd-shot "Boardroom," because it portrays every working stiff's fantasy: telling the boss to take a hike. In the

Cable
15 seconds
(SFX: Birds singing and the wind whispering.)
Prospective buyer: Does it come with cable?
Realtor: Uhh…well…
VO: New York Lotto. Hey, you never know.

Opera
30 seconds
(SFX: Male opera star singing and then stops abruptly.)
Woman: Thank you.
(SFX: Singer starts up again.)
VO: New York Lotto. Hey, you never know.

Bradford Manor
30 seconds
Tour leader: This is Bradford Hall. Notice the 19th-century Italian marble. This is the Bradford armory, the finest collection of its kind in North America. This is the Bradford library, 50,000 volumes, all extremely rare. And this is the Bradford living room. Ohh…and these are the Bradfords.
Mr. Bradford: Hey, how ya doin'? Grab a chair. We got a million of 'em. (Laughs)
VO: New York Lotto. Hey, you never know.

Backseat Driver
15 seconds
(SFX: Squealing tires)
VO: Faster…faster…faster…faster!
Announcer VO: New York Lotto. Hey, you never know.

Grand Ball
30 seconds
(SFX: Classical music in background)
Butler: Admiral and Lady Billingsly of Devonshire…Lord and Lady Atherton of Sussex…Alfred and Lady Sheffield of Dunsmoor…Bob of Buffalo.
VO: New York Lotto. Hey, you never know.

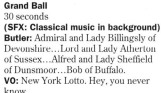

Client: New York State Lottery
Agency: DDB Needham, New York, NY
Art director: David Angelo
Copywriter: Paul Spencer
Creative director: John Staffen
PRINT SEGMENT
Photographers: Lamb & Hall ("Lamborghini," "Boat"); Neal Slavin ("BBQ," "Recliner"); Joe Baraban ("Limousine")
TV SEGMENT
Agency producer: Eric Herrmann
Production companies: Coppos Films, Limelight Productions
Directors: Brent Thomas ("Opera," "Grand Ball," "Backseat Driver"); John Lloyd ("Boardroom," "Bradford Manor," "Cable")

Boardroom
30 seconds
(SFX: Ominous music comes up and recedes.)
JP: In short, gentlemen, our capitalization plan has paid handsome dividends. Johnson here will fill you in on the details.
Johnson: Thank you, JP. Let me begin by saying…
(SFX: Door slams.)
Executive: We've been acquired!
JP: By whom? The Omega Corporation?
Executive: NO. Chuck, from the mailroom.
Chuck: Hi, boys. Mrs. Whitaker.
VO: New York Lotto. Hey, you never know.
Chuck: Coffee, Johnson.

commercial, a company's stodgy executive board is meeting in a conference room to discuss a capitalization plan. Suddenly, the door flings open and an executive blurts out: "We've been acquired!" The shocked board discovers the source of the takeover is not their competitor, the Omega Corporation, but rather, "Chuck from the mailroom." Chuck then saunters into the room with a smug look on his face. "The spot hit it perfectly because it's not just about wealth, it's about the power

that wealth gives you," Spencer says.

The campaign got a wealth of positive feedback, and is credited with ending declining sales, with a 9.63 increase from 1991 to 1992. Focus groups also reported to have an increased awareness of Lotto from 86 per cent in 1991 to 92 per cent in 1992. In addition, the campaign had a spillover effect in encouraging people to play other lottery games.

Built on the theme "If it's important to you, you'll find it in Time," this print and television campaign for the newsweekly via Fallon McElligott takes current news events and personalizes them for readers. Through the use of bold images and authoritative copy, the campaign shoves race, abortion, starvation and politics under your nose and dares you to look away.

This aggressive approach contrasts sharply with the magazine's previous campaign in the early '90s, which, with its slogan, "Make Time for Time," seemed to be an almost apologetic plea for reader attention. The new campaign needed to add some urgency to the mix. "People had come to believe that news magazines are irrelevant—something their grandmother reads," explains Fallon copywriter Phil Hanft, who teamed with art director Bob Brihn on the campaign. "But rather than saying Time is relevant, we decided to show it, through the cover stories."

To carry this off, print and TV spots play off major issues of the day, a tack that gave the advertising a look both timely and timeless. ("Opportunistic" ads promoting single issues were also created.) This approach earned the campaign high praise from Advertising Age ad critic Bob Garfield, who named it the top magazine campaign of 1993. In the March 1, 1993 issue, he writes: "[It] is the most powerful consumer-magazine campaign you are likely ever to see, combining provocative single-issue promotion with

SINCE THE FALL OF COMMUNISM, YUGOSLAVIA IS MORE RED THAN EVER. For years Communism was the straightjacket that held this historically volatile region together. But times change and so does TIME. Today, TIME not only brings you the week's news, but also gives you a closer look at how it affects you. Considering the first shot of WWI was fired in Bosnia, we'd say this bloody civil war on the other side of the globe is fairly close to home. *If it's important to you, you'll find it in TIME.*

No. *Come on.* **No.** *Please.* **No.** *What's wrong?* **Nothing.** *Then come on.* **No.** *It'll be great.* **No.** *I know you want to.* **No I don't.** *Yes, you do.* **No.** *Well, I do.* **Please stop it.** *I know you'll like it.* **No.** *Come on.* **I said no.** *Do you love me?* **I don't know.** *I love you.* **Please don't.** *Why not?* **I just don't want to.** *I bought you dinner, didn't I?* **Please stop.** *Come on, just this once.* **No.** *But I need it.* **Don't.** *Come on.* **No.** *Please.* **No.** *What's wrong?* **Nothing.** *Then come on.* **No.** *It'll be great.* **Please stop.** *I know you need it too.* **Don't.** *Come on.* **I said no.** *But I love you.* **Stop.** *I gotta have it.* **I don't want to.** *Why not?* **I just don't.** *Are you frigid?* **No.** *You gotta loosen up.* **Don't.** *It'll be good.* **No it won't.** *Please.* **Don't.** *But I need it.* **No.** *I need it bad.* **Stop it.** *I know you want to.* **No. Don't.** *Come on.* **No.** *Please.* **No.** *What's wrong?* **Nothing.** *Then come on.* **No.** *It'll be great.* **Stop.** *Come on.* **No.** *I really need it.* **Stop.** *You have to.* **Stop.** *No, you stop.* **No.** *Take your clothes off.* **No.** *Shut up and do it. Now.*

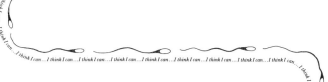

The dialogue is fictional, but date rape is not.

WHEN THE MAN OF YOUR DREAMS BECOMES YOUR WORST NIGHTMARE. Date rape is one of those cover stories that over 24 million people couldn't ignore. In fact, it ignited a national debate. It's the kind of thing TIME does. Stories that engage the reader on a more personal level by addressing issues that touch their lives. Now, can your clients really afford to miss out on reader involvement and numbers like that?

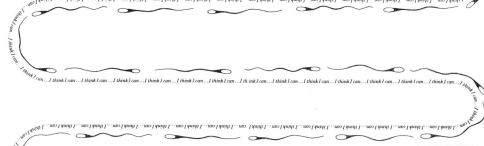

I think I can…I think I can…I think I can…I think I can…I think I can…I think I can…I think I can…I think I can…I think I can…I think I can…I think I can…I think I can…I think I can…I think I can…I think I can…

THE LITTLE ENGINE THAT COULDN'T. Fifteen years ago if one partner was infertile the other partner was out of luck. But times changes and so does TIME. Today, we still give you the news of the week. But we also tell you how the news and important issues, like curing infertility, affect you on a personal level. Call it news. Call it perspective. If it's important to you, you'll find it in TIME.

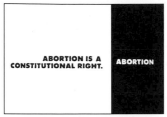

Roe vs. Wade
30 seconds
VO: No matter which side of the
abortion issue you're on, we've got
news for you.
VO: It may already be decided.
VO: Why Roe v. Wade is moot.
VO: If it's important to you, you'll find
it in Time.

The Angry Voter
30 seconds
(SFX: Typing sound)
FVO: Congress votes itself
$23 thousand pay raise.
FVO: S & L's bailed out at taxpayer
expense.
FVO: Unemployment hits 8-year high.
FVO: Congress bounces thousands of
bad checks.
Anncr VO: Last March, Time
reported a major shift in voter attitudes.
Anncr VO: We just thought you'd like
to know you're not alone.
Anncr VO: The Angry Voter.
Anncr VO: If it's important to you, you'll
find it in Time.

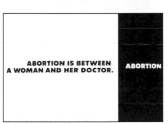

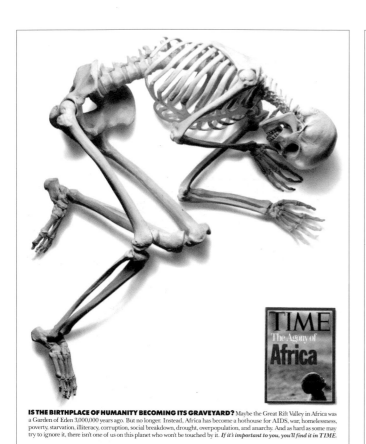

IS THE BIRTHPLACE OF HUMANITY BECOMING ITS GRAVEYARD? Maybe the Great Rift Valley in Africa was a Garden of Eden 3,000,000 years ago. But no longer. Instead, Africa has become a hothouse for AIDS, war, homelessness, poverty, starvation, illiteracy, corruption, social breakdown, drought, overpopulation, and anarchy. And as hard as some may try to ignore it, there isn't one of us on this planet who won't be touched by it. *If it's important to you, you'll find it in TIME.*

DOES GOD HAVE A FAVORITE COLOR? It seems unlikely. Yet when the Church of England allowed women into the priesthood, traditionalists looked on with alarm. Many Christians argue that Jesus himself instituted the male priesthood with 12 male Apostles. Others say the church hurts its cause by denying women leadership. Right now only a miracle can bring the two sides together. We'll keep you posted. *If it's important to you, you'll find it in TIME.*

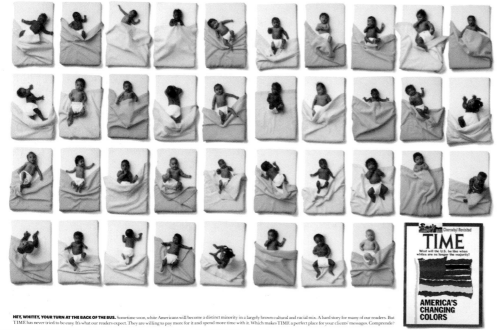

HEY, WHITEY, YOUR TURN AT THE BACK OF THE BUS. Sometime soon, white Americans will become a distinct minority in a largely brown cultural and racial mix. A hard story for many of our readers. But TIME has never tried to be easy. It's what our readers expect. They are willing to pay more for it and spend more time with it. Which makes TIME a perfect place for your clients' messages. Comprende?

what cumulatively is image-building of staggering impact."

The print portion of the campaign, aimed at media buyers, broke in March 1992 in ad weeklies and The Wall Street Journal. The ads took the cover subject and dramatized it graphically. For example, a cover story about Africa's multitude of health, starvation and overpopulation problems was illustrated with a human skeleton crouched in the fetal position. Another issue about the Balkan war features a vast field of white stained with droplets of blood-red ink. Copy reads: "Considering the first shot of

WWI was fired in Bosnia, we'd say this bloody civil war on the other side of the globe is fairly close to home." The impact of the graphic images in both print and television portions of the campaign was crucial to its effectiveness, says Hanft. "We knew when we took this approach that our ads had to be more interesting than the covers," he explains. "Otherwise the focus would be on the cover, not on the ads."

The television portion, with a $10 million-plus budget, broke four months later and increased the intensity. In one spot for the cover story "The Angry Voter," the image of a smiley-face button was borrowed from the cover illustration. As the commercial unfolds, the smiley face begins to frown, then reddens into a rage as a voiceover recites a laundry list of national ills, such as unemployment, Congressional pay raises and the budget deficit. Another spot literally demonstrates opposing sides in the abortion battle with black and white sides of the screen pushing the other. All spots close with a quick-cut montage of various Time covers backed by a sound effect of a motorized camera shutter.

The campaign wisely follows an old journalistic credo: "Show, don't tell." This approach makes the magazine's subject matter irresistible. In Garfield's words, "Whether the subject is Ross Perot or date rape, the ads find the essential drama in every story they sell."

Colorado River
30 seconds
(SFX: Toilet flush)
VO: As the water of the Colorado River goes…so go the Western states…and as the Western states go…
(SFX: Toilet flush)
VO: …so goes the country. We just thought you'd like to know. The Colorado…
Anncr VO: If it's important to you, you'll find it in Time.

Client: Time Magazine
Agency: Fallon McElligott, Minneapolis, MN
Art director: Bob Brihn
Copywriter: Phil Hanft
Creative director: Pat Burnham
PRINT SEGMENT
Photographer: Joe Lampi/Dublin Productions, Minneapolis, MN
Typographer: Bob Blewett
TV SEGMENT
Agency Producer: Judy Brink
Production company: Young & Co., Minneapolis, MN
Director: Eric Young
Animation: Tom Larson, Bruce McFarlan/Reelworks

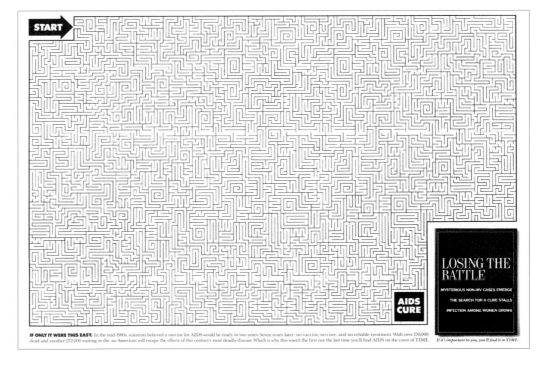

"Headhunters have a bad reputation," understates art director Nick Cohen. This negative perception is duly noted by the Creative Register, a New York executive search firm that specializes in placing advertising creatives. That's why the company allowed Cohen and copywriter/partner Ty Montague the liberty of comparing recruiters to the "common leech" in its own advertisements. Formerly known as the Junior Register, the company wanted a humorous ad campaign to introduce its broader scope, while distinguishing itself from the legions of industry glad-handers who have "nothing whatsoever to do with advertising," says Cohen.

The print campaign, which ran in Art Direction magazine, was completed as a freelance assignment in 1991 by Cohen and Montague before they departed Ogilvy & Mather to open Mad Dogs & Englishmen, a Greenwich Village boutique whose client roster now includes The Village Voice, Family Circle magazine, MTV, and Kenneth Cole Unlisted.

"Common Leech" is illustrated with a scientific line drawing of the blood-sucking Hirudinea, with copy describing how the parasite uses its "razor-sharp teeth" to attach itself to a host and gorge on blood. "If this reminds you of your headhunter," it reads, "give us a call." This ad drew such a positive response that it caused operational problems, since the firm's phone lines became flooded with many unqualified job-seekers. So

Mad Dogs hastily followed up with a second ad, which bluntly aimed to weed out the hacks from the high-end creatives. This ad features a stinking pile of excrement identified as "Ca Ca." Copy skewers hackneyed recent advertising slogans, suggesting that if a reader is the creative genius behind such lines as "Don't hate me because I'm beautiful" or "He loves my mind and he drinks Johnny Walker," then he or she should "Get on your Pontiac and ride."

Although the ad worked to effectively intimidate the unwelcome, the company did not wish to earn an arrogant reputation. So a third ad, "Perfect Suicide," empathizes with creatives who literally feel that they are in dead-end jobs. The ad is illustrated with a handsaw and describes many methods of suicide, including "hanging, electrocution...long falls onto unyielding surfaces," and, most notably, remaining "far too long in a dead-end job." Since Cohen and Montague were writing the ad as moonlighters preparing to depart their day jobs, this message truly came from the heart. "There's nothing more miserable than being in a job you don't enjoy," says Cohen.

Fig 1. Hirudinea.

THE COMMON LEECH attaches itself to its unwitting host by means of a powerful suction cup. With its razor sharp teeth, it then makes a deep incision and begins to feed. It cannot be removed without risking serious injury. Finally, gorged with blood, it tears itself free and swims off in search of its next victim. If this reminds you of your headhunter, give us a call. THE CREATIVE REGISTER. Advertising Talent Scouts. (212) 533-3676.

Fig 1. Ca Ca.

DON'T HATE ME because I'm beautiful. I'm not a doctor, but I play one on TV. Did somebody say deal? A double pleasure is waiting for you, tra la la la. I liked it so much I bought the company. Colt 45, works every time. He loves my mind <u>and</u> he drinks Johnny Walker. If any of this reminds you of your portfolio, please get on your Pontiac and ride. THE CREATIVE REGISTER. Advertising Talent Scouts. (212) 533 3676.

Fig 1. A bit messy.

THE PERFECT SUICIDE should be quiet, painless and above all, neat. This rules out many time-honored methods, including guns, knives, hanging, electrocution and long falls onto unyielding surfaces. One excellent method is a strong tea made from poisonous toadstools. Another popular, but particularly gruesome method is to stay far too long in a dead end job. THE CREATIVE REGISTER. Advertising Talent Scouts. (212) 533-3676.

Client: The Creative Register
Agency: Mad Dogs & Englishmen, New York, NY
Art director: Nick Cohen
Copywriter: Ty Montague
Creative directors: Nick Cohen, Ty Montague

The Everlast name has been a fixture in the boxing ring for many rounds. When Goldsmith/Jeffrey landed the Everlast Activewear account in 1988, they instantly realized the brand's gritty authenticity would pack its strongest marketing punch. The agency created an award-winning print campaign that taunted fashion-conscious pseudo-athletes who traipse around the gym in neon-bright warm-up suits. Ads were dominated by the familiar bold, bowtie-shaped logo followed by headlines set in tiny Courier type with such messages as, "Why didn't we do an ad that tries to sell you a 'Lifestyle'? We assumed you already had one."

A follow-up campaign in 1991 needed to maintain that irreverent attitude and this time also to show the clothing. Scheduled to break during a tough retail market period, the campaign needed not only to create interest among the target audience of young men, but also to raise confidence levels among retailers. Ads for the menswear ran in consumer and trade magazines, as well as in kiosks in shopping malls to reach consumers en route to stores and retailers with businesses nearby.

Three ads from the '91 campaign were chosen by judges to appear in this Casebook. Each one unabashedly champions male virility. A soiled, sweaty sweatshirt appears in one black-and-white ad with the headline: "This is not one of those scented ads. Good thing." Another features a crane's spindly legs poking out from a pair of gym shorts, and

the headline: "You may never have the legs of a bodybuilder. Great shorts, however, are readily available." Celebrity endorsers are slammed in a third ad featuring a dazed-looking manikin. The headline asks: "Who needs to see another celebrity jock?"

Apparently, consumers and retailers don't need to. Everlast Activewear sales increased 10 per cent after the campaign broke. In addition, many retailers contacted the company to add the line at a time when most of them were scrambling to get out of their present contracts. The posters were also so popular among consumers that they were stolen from mall kiosks.

The success of the brand's image, however, owes much to its heritage, says agency principal Gary Goldsmith, who art-directed the campaign. "There's so much artificiality out there, with brands like Ralph Lauren trying to create an old-world image," he says. "That's pure fabrication. This is real."

You may never have the legs of a body builder. Great shorts, however, are readily available.

Client: Everlast Activewear
Agency: Goldsmith/Jeffrey, New York, NY
Art director: Gary Goldsmith
Copywriter: Ty Montague
Creative director: Gary Goldsmith
Photographer: Steve Hellerstein

Blink your eyes and you will nearly miss the fleeting mini-dramas flashing by in these black-and-white commercials for the Utah Short Film & Video Festival. Each :15 spot borrows a split-second clip from vintage serial movies—an exploding zeppelin, a gun fight, a terrified man—to send up the focus of the annual event held by the Utah Film & Video Center in Salt Lake City.

"Our first thought was to use midgets," jokes David Hughes, a graphic designer at Williams & Rockwood, who with agency art director Darren Elwood wrote, art-directed and edited the campaign as a freelance project. "But the problem really solved itself." The festival attracts the work of independent filmmakers from across the country, who enter their shorts in categories such as industrial videos, documentaries, feature films and advertising. Throughout the year, the Center continues to support filmmakers by obtaining grants and holding educational programs.

In previous years, the Film Center advertised the festival with staid, network-produced television commercials featuring a still shot of the logo with a voiceover. Their posters were similarly uninspired, says Hughes, consisting of the festival logo and dates on neon-colored paper. Initially, the Center asked Hughes and Elwood to create a new poster, but the team persuaded them to add broadcast to the mix. "We thought of it as an opportunity to upgrade their presence,"

says Hughes. "It's a fairly well-respected festival, but it never got any notice because they were tacking up these Day-Glo posters."

With a shoestring budget and donated editing equipment, the team searched for the clips through dozens of reels of old movie serials from the 1940s and 1950s borrowed from a local television station, which held the rights to them. Once they had the footage, they added a film leader from an old driver's education film to the beginning of each spot. At the end, they added titles with information about the festival.

In addition, the team produced a black-and-white poster featuring the image of a bare-chested man with a film leader projected on—what else?—his boxer shorts. The photo was shot by local photographer Dan Arsenault, whose volunteer model was a local triathlete with modeling aspirations. Design credits for the poster and the commercials are given to the League of Bald-Headed Men, which Hughes explains is an ersatz name he and Elwood came up with for the purpose of entering awards shows. The name is a tribute to an intelligence division in the 1960s TV comedy series "Get Smart."

After the campaign ran locally, attendance doubled at the modest little festival, from 100 in 1991 to 200 in 1992.

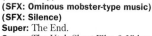

Stare
15 seconds
(SFX: Bleep)
(SFX: Ominous mobster-type music)
(SFX: Silence)
Super: The End.
Super: The Utah Short Film & Video Festival.
Super: June 15–20. At the Utah Film & Video Center.
Super: Don't miss it.

Client: Utah Film & Video Center
Agency: Williams & Rockwood, Salt Lake City, UT
Art directors: Darren Elwood, David Hughes
Copywriters: Darren Elwood, David Hughes
Creative director: Scott Rockwood
PRINT SEGMENT
Photographer: Dan Arsenault
TV SEGMENT
Production company: The League of Bald-Headed Men

United Parcel Service's 64,000 trucks are brown, boxy and compact—just like many of the 10 million packages they deliver each day. The trucks are so familiar on the roads that it's only logical that the creative team at Ammirati & Puris would grab the chance to manipulate the familiar icon in UPS's advertising. "People know UPS for those trucks," says A&P copywriter David Wojdyla. "Fortunately, the client doesn't treat it like a holy icon you can't touch."

In this consumer and trade magazine print campaign aimed at shipping managers in small- to medium-sized businesses, the truck plays a central role in visual puns that emphasize specific attributes of the company, such as speed, reliability or coverage. This sprucing-up strategy works to position the country's leading package delivery company as one that is not only "big, fast and efficient," says creative director Tod Seisser, but that is also "a living, breathing company that gives a damn." One ad whose head reads "Just this once, we'd like to give our vehicles the image they deserve" features the truck emblazoned with orange and red racecar flames.

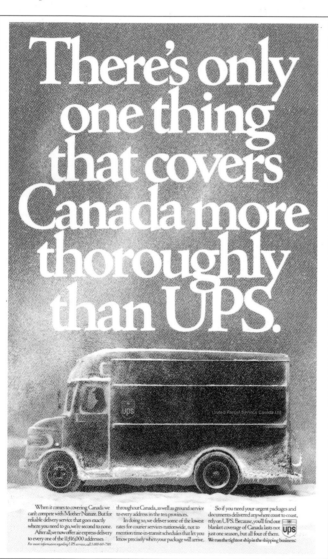

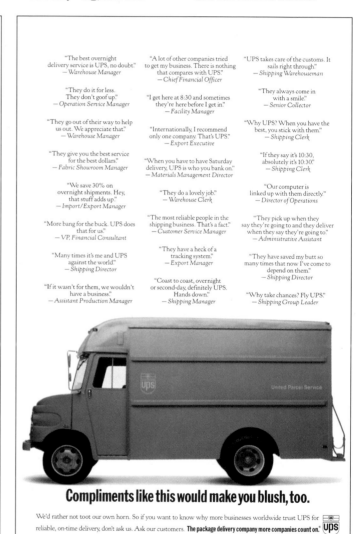

Just this once, we'd like to give our vehicles the image they deserve.

Of course you won't see any of our drivers making deliveries in anything like this. You will however notice the speed at which our ground service works.

Quite simply, UPS offers the fastest scheduled ground delivery serving the forty-eight states today. In fact, of the ten million packages we deliver each day, four million are overnight ground deliveries. And when you couple that with our well proven record for on-time reliability, you can rest assured that your packages will consistently arrive at the time they are scheduled to arrive. All within the legal speed limits.

So why ship with anyone else but UPS. After all, with 64,000 vehicles on the road and eighty-four years of experience, it's no wonder our service is what some might call, well, up to speed. **UPS**

We run the tightest ship in the shipping business.

Likewise, a testimonial ad with 24 quotes from shipping managers shows the UPS truck painted flamingo pink above the headline "Compliments like this would make you blush, too."

Apparently, the latter headline rang true for the creative team while that ad was being created. Although the pink truck was supposed to be covered with a tarp for its short drive to Lamb & Hall, the Los Angeles photography studio, it wasn't. The spectacle elicited a predictable barrage of hoots and whistles from neighboring drivers.

Every day, ten million ground packages arrive in this shape.

Each day, UPS is entrusted with delivering more packages than any other ground delivery service. But when you take into consideration our well proven record for on-time reliability, it's no small wonder that over a million businesses rely upon our familiar brown package cars.

In fact, with as many as 64,000 vehicles on the road daily, we offer the fastest, most efficient ground delivery service to every single address in the lower forty-eight states. Knowing all that, it's quite easy to understand why UPS continues to be the most widely used ground carrier.

So when you send your package with UPS, you'll not only know when it will arrive but also exactly what shape it'll arrive in. **UPS**

We run the tightest ship in the shipping business.

Client: United Parcel Service
Agency: Ammirati & Puris, New York, NY
Art directors: Nan Hutchinson, David Berger, Russlyn Mills, Curt Johnson
Copywriters: Larry Goldstein, David Wojdyla
Creative directors: Ralph Ammirati, Tom Nelson, Tod Seisser
Photographer: Lamb & Hall, Los Angeles

Boulevard Brewing Company used to regard advertising with the same disdain it had for warm Budweiser. It simply had no taste for either brew. And why should it? The five-year-old Kansas City, Missouri, microbrewery sells every drop of the beer it makes for local consumption. Its four beers—Pale Ale, Wheat Beer, Bully! Porter, and Irish Ale—are the toast of the town, which is already on the map for its copious consumption of beef barbecue (you need something to wash it down with). The brewery also has a limited ability to produce and distribute its product, since it rents space in the delivery trucks of a national producer. The creatives at Valentine-Radford had their work cut out for them. Not only did they need to sell Boulevard an advertising concept, they had to sell them on the concept of advertising.

The agency seized Boulevard's ambivalent attitude and translated it into an irreverent image campaign that matched the brewery's personality. Ads for print and outdoor that shrug and say, "Drink it before someone else does," and "We brew it. We drink it. We bottle what's left" exhibit the same boozy apathy one might observe during last call at a bar. Copywriter Mary McPhail sensed this approach was on target seconds after the pitch was made to the client. After the creative team showed the work, she says, one Boulevard exec exclaimed, "Oh boy, can we do that on T-shirts for our employees?"

Initially, the team had considered showing multiple,

In early comps for Boulevard, Lee St. James toyed with a variety of contemporary electronic typefaces, but eventually fell for the quick-and-dirty allure of the Dymo label maker.

© BOULEVARD BEER 1993

© BOULEVARD BEER 1993

Employee T-shirts were a byproduct of the ad campaign.

beer-related images, such as wheat, bottles, and the brewery entrance, to appeal to the young, upscale target audience, but those boards were rejected before the pitch because they were weighted with "too much visual for the headlines," says McPhail.

Once they had the go-ahead, McPhail and art directors Lee St. James and Dan Lutz worked to fine-tune the visuals. Their final approach was spare and clean with simple product shots by photographer Ron Berg. The typeface used needed to fully embody the spirit of the copy, or, in McPhail's words, "to find the proper degree of insouciance." After toying with several contemporary typefaces, St. James reached for a Dymo label maker and started clicking. "We liked its casual, almost throwaway immediacy," he explains. "The decision to use it liberated us from adland, and that was all we needed."

They did not take that freedom for granted. To McPhail, creating an ad campaign for a client who has little incentive to sell was as refreshing as a frosted mug of lager. "When will I ever get the chance again to do a non-ad ad?" she asks.

Client: Boulevard Brewing Co.
Agency: Valentine-Radford, Kansas City, MO
Art directors: Lee St. James, Dan Lutz
Copywriter: Mary McPhail
Creative directors: Gary Brahl, Lee St. James
Photographer: Ron Berg

Porsche

How do you sell luxury sports cars in the middle of a recession? Address the buyer's pretensions and feelings of guilt. Or, as Fallon McElligott art director Bob Barrie puts it, create an aura of "accessible elitism."

Stakes were high for the Minneapolis agency when it landed the Porsche account in the early 1990s. Sales had plunged from 30,471 in 1986 to 4133 in 1992. Fallon had to convince the target audience that by plunking down close to six figures for a car, they would be getting both a sexy driving machine and a sensible investment. Image-driven television spots took care of the sexy part. This newspaper print campaign aimed to increase traffic at dealerships.

Targeted to wealthy males over 40, this retail campaign running in local newspapers had hundreds of executions to cover a wide variety of selling points, from price and resale value to performance and style. Some of the ads position the cars as a good investment while winking at potential buyers' guilt feelings. One ad headlined "Don't feel selfish. In a few decades you can pass it on to your children" goes on to say: "True, a sports car may seem like an indulgence. But with its timeless styling, remarkable durability, and exceptional resale value, a new Porsche 911 Carerra is virtually guilt-free."

Obviously, the campaign is fueled by attitude with a heavy dose of testosterone. One ad for the 911 Turbo, for example, reads: "It's not a statement. It's a hand

gesture." Body copy further enhances the message: "With an awe-inspiring 315-horsepower engine and a shape more akin to a rocket than an automobile, the Porsche 911 Turbo makes a very strong statement indeed. We now have this very rare automobile on hand."

Unfortunately, the same could not be said of Fallon McElligott. Although their Porsche work won scores of awards, Porsche fired the agency in March 1993, hired Goodby, Berlin & Silverstein, San Francisco, and increased their ad budget by 50 per cent.

Client: Porsche Cars North America
Agency: Fallon McElligott, Minneapolis, MN
Art director: Bob Barrie
Copywriter: Bruce Bildsten
Creative director: Pat Burnham
Photographer: Vic Huber, Shawn Michienzi

Don't feel selfish. In a few decades you can pass it on to your children.

True, a sportscar may seem an indulgence. But with its timeless styling, remarkable durability, and exceptional resale value, a new Porsche 911 Carrera is virtually guilt-free.

PORSCHE

It's not a statement. It's a hand gesture.

With an awe-inspiring 315-horsepower engine and a shape more akin to a rocket than an automobile, the Porsche 911 Turbo makes a very strong statement indeed. We now have this very rare automobile on hand.

PORSCHE